CONFLICT INTELLIGENCE *Quotient*

"Conflict-IQ™"

D1736877

The Missing Piece to Turbocharge
Conscious Leaders' and Organizations'
Emotional Intelligence

Yvette Durazo, MA, ACC

Table of Content

Prologue

—

Purpose of This Book

The book is inspired by my passion to serve, educate, and contribute to the field of Alternative Dispute Resolution (ADR) and to the development of organizational employees and their leaders. These professionals, in various ways, shape the organizations in our communities. There is a need to educate people on the beautiful field of ADR because of its value to organizations and society. ADR techniques can transform humanity and make them realize that being punitive or divisive is not the only way to deal with human conflict. Every person can manage or resolve human conflict without it ending in the need to opt for costly legal options. Interestingly, not all disputes may be resolved; however, those that do not have the potential to be resolved amicably can be managed.

The book was also created from my professional experience of having the privilege of working with many professionals in the past 11 years, doing consulting work with educational institutions, non-profit organizations, and organizations throughout California. Also, by contributing my time in many associations serving on the Boards, Committees, and Cohorts, and also attending many networking events, I learned how many professionals, human resources, lawyers attempting to be mediators, and consultants lack adequate tools to resolve human organizational problems. Each time I heard them talk about how they had resolved conflicts, I felt sorry for those who may have been at the receiving end of their service. I realized how negatively they may have impacted people's experiences with their rather myopic knowledge of conflict resolution as a disciplinary process. Furthermore, when I heard stories from people around me who received relatively poor mediation service from inadequately trained mediators, I realized the necessity to make this book happen.

Finally, although this book has been in the works in my mind since 2014, I felt that now is the time to bring this book to as many hands as I can, as we are all collectively dealing with a problematic universal COVID-19 pandemic, political division, and social justice movement on the streets of America. I made it relatable and easy for anyone to read and understand. There is so much uncertainty in the world today, with people living in fear and isolation, and I only hope my book helps transform people's approach to communicate with one another and embrace positive approaches to conflict resolution.

One thing I can assure you is that the topic of conflict resolution is not a "soft" skill that can be learned after spending a few hours watching a video, a live or online workshop, or after reading a few books; instead, it is a life skill that embraces knowledge from sociology, psychology, anthropology, humanities, and experiential processes to lead you to be competent at any given conflicting human situation. It is a life skill that is needed every day in our lives, as long as humans are in this world. As we interact with other people around us, there is a tendency for conflicts to arise at different points. This is because each of us is different, from different backgrounds, personalities, experiences, and perceptions about life and living.

The information contained within the book will help you improve your awareness about the importance of learning alternative ways to resolve human conflicts. It also gives you the opportunity to expand your conflict resolution skills while helping you understand that conflict does not get resolved with the same technique, methodology, or skill. Furthermore, you will realize that conflict resolution takes into cognizance emotional intelligence, behavioral transformation, as well as other tools and knowledge needed to put you in charge of the conflict as you resolve it amicably.

Please allow me to reiterate that not all conflicts can be resolved. However, they can be managed with the right resources and approach.

Acknowledgments

—

I am grateful to God as I feel that I am doing His work stated in the bible verse **Matthew 5:9** "Blessed are the Peacemakers." I am thankful for the hardships I've endured throughout my life. They have made me stronger and more resilient. As a working, single mother, I've withstood and overcome the pressures that accompany that role. Along the way, there have been other factors that contributed additional burdens, such as being the first generation of my family to achieve a master's degree and coping with health challenges. As a Hispanic woman, I have experienced gender and cultural inequities in the workforce. As a professional, I experienced first-hand how poorly trained managers with zero or negligible people skills can adversely affect a person's health and mental well-being.

I also want to thank everyone who has contributed to the experience positively or negatively that has brought me to this point and for helping me garner knowledge and life wisdom, enough to share in this book and thus make the world a better place for all. Life has taught me so many things; I figured the best way to share with others would be by putting it in a book filled with knowledge, experiences, and tools needed for peaceful conflict resolution. This is a book especially for professionals who manage people and leaders, consultants, coaches, human resources, and anyone else looking to resolve conflicts.

I want to acknowledge my mother, who gifted me with the aptitude to be strong in the eye of adversity, and my father for being my first and most crucial, conscious business mentor who always put his employees first before profit.

To my daughter Frida for her healthy scientific leadership mind and to my son, Cristobal, for reminding me that creativity and people skills can rule the world and the people's hearts.

And...

To my grandchildren, Calif and Kalo Kalel, for giving me the means to get healthy doses of oxytocin- the happy hormone of creation of bonding, the food to my heart and soul on those weekends we spend together.

Thank you to all my mentors who have seen the light in me, have opened the doors for me, and have spent lots of hours developing me, shaping me, disrupting my thinking, and supporting my passion for being of service to others.

In grace, thank you!

Introduction

—

The phrase "I QUIT" is one of the most dreaded words an employee can utter when pushed to the edge at their workplace. You must have heard before the saying, "employees do not leave companies; they leave bad and abusive bosses or leaders." This happens in organizations more often than not, but the reasons it happens are overlooked too many times by the leaders without questioning how much a bad leader is really costing the organization in turnaround cost and low morale that leads to mediocre productivity.

One of the most controversial and proliferating reasons employees and leaders alike are unhappy is when human conflict shadows the organization's culture. Indeed, conflict is an inevitable situation that never seems to leave humans alone since the inception of time. It is only normal for conflict to follow us like a swarm of bees to a honeycomb. Wherever there are people, then there will be conflict. This case is usually because of the disparity in cultural backgrounds, social status, values, beliefs, ideologies, and other differentiating factors.

Organizations have now become a melting pot for culture and diverse people. Therefore, conflict sticks its head in places where humans interact with one another. This book uncovers the positive side of conflict through conflict intelligence "Conflict-IQ™".

The sustainability and success of many organizations hinge on the effective management of conflicts among employees and leaders. Conflict intelligence is the key for people to properly thrive in organizations with a diverse and changing environment. The sustainability and success of many organizations hinge on the effective management of conflict among employees and leaders. For people to properly thrive in a diverse environment, conflict intelligence is the key. The subject of conflict intelligence has peaked in recent times, with more people interested in the areas that ensure organizations stop losing money and harness the resources available to them to develop.

This book takes a deep dive into human conflict in the workplace and why the author's company was named "Unitive" Consulting. The methodology she unveiled, called Conflict-IQ™, was discovered after working with thousands of professionals and their organizations in developing harmonious, diverse, and inclusive workplace relationships. It starts with a gradual trend of examining the human state's fundamental concepts before transcending into the complex topic of consciousness and how conflict intelligence could be the missing key to edifying the great leaders that are missing in many of today's organizations. Each chapter is a continuation of the previous one, which aids readers' comprehension.

This book will teach others how to open the doorway of becoming conflict resolution competent, how you can employ these skills, and how having Conflict-IQ™ employees improves organizations.

The book takes a closer look into emotional intelligence and conflict intelligence and the effective combination of both forms of IQ.

1

The Unitive Way

"No problem can be solved from the same level of consciousness that created it."

— *Albert Einstein*

The Unitive Way represents a new approach or pathway to heighten people's thinking and reactions, to significantly enhance their abilities to relate with other humans in positive and intelligent ways. This approach augments people's emotional intelligence to become smarter in approaching human conflict. My consulting business name was inspired by the meaning of the word "UNITIVE," which signifies to transform organizational leaders to a state of consciousness in where not only they can become exemplified leaders to lead with integrity, honesty, empathy, inclusion, and dignity, but to also be in a unitive state in their homes, their communities and in society. Human conflict can be experienced through each of us in an intrapersonal conflict

(conflict with oneself) and intrapersonal conflict (conflict between two people). Albert Einstein's famous quote explains that conflict cannot be resolved from the same level of thinking from which it was born. In this chapter, you will learn about the Unitive Way, how the concept was born, why this approach can be the precursor to augment people's emotional intelligence, and overall a good factor predictor of success in the workplace and organizational line.

A host of factors contribute to an organization's success in the holistic approach and the individualistic line. The advancement of technology today has made organizations take different course levels in creating a dynamic, systematic, and organized process that is in line with the cultural, social, economic, and psychological aspects of life. The need for businesses to creatively implement innovations that will improve their business in all areas revolves around each member that embodies each organization. In a bid to actualize the set goals, there is a call for all individuals to take on the leadership role in positioning their organization as a leading brand in whatever niche they specialize in. The reality is that traditional educational systems still, to this day, lack the fundamental teachings around values and skills that are vital for professionals to become influential leaders.

The constant acquisition of skills in the workforce is imperative for the growth and development of an organization. It goes without saying that unless an employee takes their initiative to invest in self-develop efforts, the organization could potentially end up with a toxic work environment.

Therefore, this results in high employee turnover, absenteeism, unmotivated employees, lack of innovation, and unproductivity. There is a risk to organizations when only considering leaders who only ascend to the corporate ladder because of the business knowledge and do not possess the skills required to explore different levels of consciousness, self-mastery, and self-transformation. A Unitive Way leader can have the capacity to create an excellent working culture, be an influencer-leader, and valuable community leader. The synergy between skills acquisition and consciousness development makes it easy for employees to transition into realms of leadership faster and effectively. Leaders that create hostile work environments have profound effects on organizations' bottom line. You see, humans are in part a by-product of what they learn from others through social transmission; biases, patterns of thinking, values, beliefs, and especially the way we interact with one another, all this gets glued in our minds by the age of seven. Psychologist Sigmund Freud coined the idea that people shape their personalities at such a young age.

Nevertheless, there are instances that the mind transitions form of thought in our minds as we move through life. Our understanding of some ideas and issues might change, depending on internal and external experiences as we progress through life, which calls for the need to develop a higher consciousness level. It is such a phenomenon when particular thought patterns, behavior, and values begin to alter or heighten based on social interactions. People can also go through a deterioration in their level of reasoning. They can also remain at the same level because of the caliber of their social interactions or the need to interact socially. There is hope that people can attain a level of maturity in their consciousness level where they learn different ways of relating with other people. This chapter will focus on the two categories that explain consciousness levels: consciousness based on theological theories and consciousness based on psychological development.

Theological Level of Consciousness

According to American psychologist Abraham Maslow's Hierarchy of Needs, a theory of psychological health states that fulfilling innate human needs is a priority culminating in the self-actualization of knowing your inner self. As a leader in organizations, you need to interact with your peers, seniors, and others who support your need to accomplish the organizational objectives. Leaders' capacity to understand human behavior around them to influence collaboration can come from the growth and transcendence needed in the Maslow hierarchy. It also comes from experiences gained from identifying universality, spirituality, and quality of being free to experience life in the present moment. This theory of transcendence marks that humans can thrive within themself and when involved with others, they take cognizance that something goes beyond the physical realm into the spiritual that influences one another. The aspect of transcendence pumps creative juice into the brain, and the concept of transcendence and leadership can be self-taught through life experiences or taught only if the individual has a strong motivation to learn. Imagine if people in organizations could have the capacity to carefully sink into a state of deep consciousness to gain peace and clarity needed for influence, have creativity, focus, and productivity. Through inner peace, one grows in the development of personal values and identity. The synergy that occurs when the mind unites with divine intelligence leads to a greater level of self-realization. Imagine having leaders in an organization that are ascending higher levels of awareness and self-fulfillment, combining their personalities and consciousness to actualize the company's goals and objectives. In retrospect, individuals can barely identify their strengths and weaknesses without connecting to a higher level of consciousness, thereby limiting the business's ability to grow and scale. Companies cannot function in isolation, which means each individual's collaborative effort leads to realizing company goals.

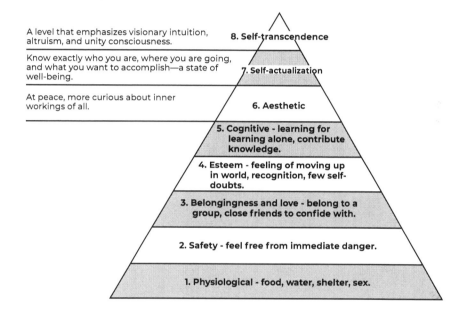

Maslow's Hierarchy of Needs

Robert Kegan is regarded as one of the most qualified scholars on the subject matter of leadership and stage development theory. According to him, leadership is a spiritual entity that can be attained only by advancing in certain levels of human consciousness needed to tackle an organization's problems. According to scholars, there are three ways of achieving self-mastery in the spiritual realm, which plays a significant role in the leadership qualities needed to move the organization forward. These ways are as follows:

1. **The Purgative Way**

2. **The Illuminative Way**

3. **The Unitive Way**

These ways of attaining self-mastery all contribute to the development of a human at different stages of life. A proper understanding of the buildup to these paths is necessary; they relate to a particular understanding of a supreme being. Anthropologists believe that the sense of belonging to a particular set of people with shared values, beliefs, and behaviors gives certain people an identity through which they can live, survive, and belonging.

The Purgative Way

The purgative way of life explains the low level of awareness by people who do not realize there are several ways to resolve conflicts or show interest in creating new ways to live. They prefer the mundane functionalities of life.

The Illuminative Way

This form of consciousness characterizes some level of

stability in adopting a more intelligent approach to life. For this level of consciousness, the individual starts to realize that there is a possibility of handling issues by applying different methods. These people are open to the idea of new changes and adaptations to a different way of life.

The Unitive Way

This is the highest spiritual disposition of the human level of consciousness. This level shows a unique understanding that everything affects anything else and involves the actions of a supreme source. It is a different form of a walk from which the people who adopt this state of awareness or level of consciousness turn away from temporal or earthly things and fix their eyes on what truly matters in life. They believe nothing else matters as a catalyst of change, doing good deeds, and not focusing on being right, rather understanding human thinking. These people belong to a strong group of believers who find inner peace due to constant communication with their inner selves and self-mastery of their thoughts and emotions. The dependence on their identity is so strong that there is absolutely nothing that goes on in their lives without them comprising their supreme being.

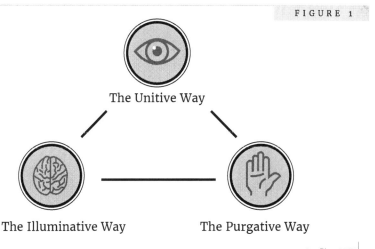

FIGURE 1

The Unitive Way

The Illuminative Way   The Purgative Way

Within these different ways of thinking, people discover their identity through social interaction and how people perceive them. The diagram below represents the relationship between the three states of perfection:

Psychological Level of Consciousness

Kegan explains that an individual has the potential to evolve in stages throughout his/her life. The stage development process defines the dynamic nature of change that transitions an individual from one level of consciousness to another. It is also essential to know that transition from one level of consciousness to another may take years to attain as it does not just happen all at once. Research shows that humans hardly regress to a previous level of consciousness; however, they may remain in that same spot until new information or life experiences break through the wall of that particular level. The figure below represents the consciousness levels:

FIGURE 1.1

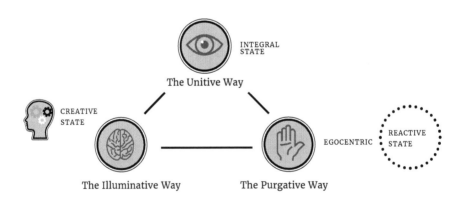

Egocentric State

This state of consciousness occurs where individuals are still trying to make sense of life's realities. The feeling of the world revolving around them they act out that disposition of their adolescent behavior. Interestingly, there is a veil covering people in a selfish state. They do not believe that changing this approach to life will aid them—unfortunately, only a small percentage of adults transit from this level of consciousness stage to the next in a lifetime. They stay stuck in the bubble that the world revolves around their needs. Some leaders and employees remain in this state. They feel that the world owes them some form of explanation whenever their expectations fail. Leaders tend to become authoritative and dictatorial by using anything to get their way. At the same time, employees play the victim card to get what they want in the organization.

Reactive State

The joy that fills people's hearts in this stage of consciousness is indescribable, as they accept you belong in that circle with them. This state characterizes belonging to a particular community of people based on your biases in life. These adults in the reactive state are referred to as "well-meaning citizens." After crossing over from adolescence, most of us get a job, which helps us identify with and interact with a particular set of people that align with our values, goals, and objectives. The thrill of being a part of a significant set of people drives them in this stage of development because they believe they have a role to play in achieving their company goals and objectives. Through the idea of belonging to a group, people in the reactive state carve an identity and a niche for themselves. An example of how people in this state identify with the roles they play in life could be employees in an advertising agency in which each employee plays a different role: copywriting; graphic designers, art directors, and team lead, all have their roles to play, and each of these employees identifies their persona with the role they play collectively. In the reactive state of development, leaders are empathetic towards their employees and are concerned about their mental, social, and even financial well-being.

On the other hand, the employee works effectively with his team members. In the reactive state, creativity is still limited as decision-making comes from the leaders. It may be hard for the individual to break free from this state and transition onto the next level of consciousness because there is the fear of losing their collective identity. In many instances, people in this reactive state believe that their only identity is their job title and company.

Creative State

In this state of consciousness, individuals follow their true calling in whatever field they choose. In many instances, they will pursue traditional education to career paths. When people acquire this creative state, age is no barrier, as they genuinely know how to do their best. They are passionate, focus, and stick with what they know how to do from an early age. People in the creative state develop leadership potentials in that field at an early stage. For instance, we have soccer stars at the summit of their careers at 21, software developer genius at the age of 12, and cryptocurrency giants at 18.

Integral State

This state is a deeper level of self-realization than the creative state of consciousness, as individuals take a closer look at their lives and uncover latent abilities. However, this stage of consciousness is where individuals are vulnerable but need to take some steps at becoming better versions of themselves.

They realize that there is still room for improvement even when it is obvious that they are doing a fantastic job. Leaders that have attained this level have become more aware of the lapses in society and strive to make amends by providing services that foster greater participation among employees to build a better future for people.

Unitive State

The unitive state manifests in individuals attaining this state a deep level of serenity in their spirit. An overwhelming stream of constant life experiences, reflection, attaining wisdom, and self-mastery is what gets people into this state of consciousness. Leadership in this state is tough to come by because they operate as global visionaries. They do not see the need to be all about the money; rather, it is always about empowering lives. These types of leaders focus on the best in people, and so they always say things like, "You can do it; I believe in you." They want to see the world flourish. In this stage of consciousness, individuals experience growth mindsets to see the world of possibilities and encourage others' growth.

Inspired by the Unitive state of being and my desire to envision a world of individuals that could ascend to this state of consciousness, is how I chose the name of my company Unitive Consulting. With the Unitive state of consciousness inspiration in mind, I developed the Unitive Way that resembles an evolution of thinking that allows us to see new possibilities, methods, and techniques to relate to one another in a harmonious spirit. The Unitive Way is a teaching method to bring individuals to a state of consciousness where they are at peace with themselves. In turn, they are at peace with others as they learn the aptitudes to become Conflict Intelligent "Conflict IQ™". Ironically, the best way to relate with others is to first find their self-identity. This is a theme that I always cover with the students I teach at various universities, and to professionals, I train in becoming Conflict Intelligent a real sense of belonging does not come until realizing your self-identity. The Unitive Way is the highest form of inner peace you attain when you relate and interact with other people using Conflict-IQ™. When you obtain self-mastery and know who you are, no one can make you feel less or more. There is a serenity that comes from this self-mastery. A quietness comes from within, making you even more creative while you experience inner happiness and reach higher levels of productivity.

The Unitive Way concept unfolds a human process of bringing individuals to a state where they are receptive and open to explore different pathways on how to relate to one another. It is an ultimate state where one can see possibilities, opportunities and welcome new experiences in life. It is an evolved state of mind, level of thinking, and inner peace. Wisdom is not to be confused with knowledge, which has to do with gathering facts and information. Learning is gathering head knowledge, while wisdom comes from understanding, insight, or experiences. The Unitive Way seeks to develop an extraordinary intelligence that does not come from knowing but rather from understanding. The individual who gets to this stage of thinking is secure and has complete peace with him/herself and others around them. The Unitive Way is where intelligence meets emotional intelligence and collides to relate to the self and others by understanding that inner and outer conflict transforms into opportunities.

My father was my first role model of who I could say was at the Unitive Way flow. What intrigued me the most was that my father was a self-made man with no formal education. I can also say that his way of being with himself and others intrigued me to pursue a personal and career journey of discovering how to find the key insights in people's minds and hearts to develop a methodology to train individuals to gain sclf-mastery in the Unitive Way. I had the privilege of spending many hours with my father at a very young age in his shop. What most fascinated me about my father was to witness how his employees trusted and respected him and were very loyal by taking good care of his business and the customers.

My father used to teach me about his business philosophy. He was a profoundly spiritual man who believed in valuing people more than things or money. His business leadership style could rightly be called "conscious business leader" or "servant leadership." He cared so deeply about other's well-being more than making a profit. After years of studying different philosophies, theology, the theory of psychology, anthropology, sociology, and business, I have become more and more passionate about contributing to the field of professional development, which impacts not only our businesses but also our communities and future generations.

Unitive Way is the culture that inspires trust with effective communication and resolution to human misunderstandings. When enacted by people, everyone feels respected and heard across all levels. It helps to clarify communication systems across cultures in a skillful, non-threatening approach. You are endorsing a level of awareness and consciousness to bring about a sense of belonging for everyone and help develop individuals with the open exchange of ideas free of cultural taboos, harmful biases, and egocentric actions.

2

The Leaky Bottom-line in Organizations

> *"Hard times make healthy people. Strong people make good times. Good times make weak people. Weak people make hard times."*
>
> — *Anonymous*

This chapter moves away from the consciousness levels explained in the previous chapter; it focuses on how conflict affects organizations' finances. Furthermore, it elucidates the essence of consciousness levels and conflict intelligence in improving revenue.

Human relationships are the basis of an organization's growth. Without a mutually beneficial relationship in the workplace, there cannot be progress. Organizations have goals and objectives that are tailored to help them actualize their vision. Leaders cannot shoulder all the organization's responsibility alone unless employees rally around them in collaboration.

With this in mind, all employees with different job roles and specifications work cohesively as independent units striving to achieve a common goal. Studies have shown that no human is an island of experience; therefore, an organization will not thrive in the isolation of ideas. Organizational leadership is responsible for establishing connected lines of communication, interaction, and relationships with people. These lines help form most of what we know and apply in our organizations today.

No organization wants to come off as having conflict among its personnel. Understandably, it is a touchy subject that affects the companies' reputation in the business community, and leaders do not want to air their problems. Still, the reality of nature is that issues emanate among employees, affecting the organization's goals and objectives. It is important to note that not all human conflict is negative. Some conflicts can be healthy for the teams in organizations. Let's explore the distinction between good and bad conflict.

There are two types of human conflict: Emotional Conflict and Cognitive Conflict. When conflict is emotional, people focus on parties involved rather than solving the issue. This type of conflict can escalate rapidly and be unpredictable. Emotional conflict can spread like wildfire and thus create toxicity in the culture of any organization. On the other hand, cognitive conflict should be embraced and encouraged in the organization because it involves focusing on ideas for resolution and not attacking one another. Cognitive conflict can have the potential of increasing workplace productivity. Emotional conflict can become expensive if it is not dealt with and transformed into a cognitive conflict. An average employee in an organization works approximately 35 to 45 hours weekly (including breaks and lunch). However, when issues arise between coworkers or among leaders and employees, the number of productive work hours diminishes greatly (BLS 2019).

Consequently, this translates to the conflict hindering employees' productivity, which eventually hampers the organization's efficiency. Dealing with stress resulting from conflict can be another factor in the leaky bottom line for organizations. According to the American Institute of Stress, employees' output diminishes to less than 3 hours per day, which results in organizations losing up to $600 per employee every week because they are dealing with workplace conflict stress. This figure is on a median salary of approximately $23.93 per hour, which can equate that an employee will not be productive for about 25 hours of the week (BLS 2020).

Furthermore, most of the ideas that enhance an organization's image and fortune involve interactions with other employees to achieve a common goal. In a more relatable situation, imagine a digital marketing company that is supposed to run an advertising campaign for a beer company as part of their plans to partner with a basketball association. The team has to go through brainstorming sessions to look for innovative ideas that will leave the clients and the audience in awe after seeing the campaign. Many things will be deliberated, from the slogan to the creative copies and then to the campaign direction. Nothing succeeds if there is no harmony in the communication and interaction levels of employees. The brainstorming will ultimately be an arena for arguments and inconclusiveness. Emotional conflict is the turmoil that brews from faulty human relationships, and that causes a leaky bottom line in organizations.

There is no place where humans gather that conflicts will not occur. Conflicts can arise due to the disparities in our consciousness levels. Even if your employees are all siblings in one hypothetical large family, there would still be conflict. However, organizations' ability to mitigate disputes and properly make resolutions is an added advantage to any business. Conflicts do not come up suddenly; it results from several minute issues that build up until employees cannot take it anymore. When conflict manifests into a visual form, it starts to get the Human Resource departments' attention, which most likely does not offer the carrot-stick approach to resolving human conflict.

There can also be conflict arising between the organization and the customers. Without customers, an organization cannot make profits. Customers are stakeholders in any business; and thus, the conflict left unresolved between an organization and a customer can cause a significant crisis, consequently leading to a leaky bottom line and smear on the company's image.

Not all conflicts are harmful as early established; some have a way of putting the organization in order. Does this seem counterintuitive? Not really. Some conflicts help identify a company's weaknesses and empower them to take prompt action. Issues sometimes help refine the organization and create a better environment for the employees to perform their duties more proficiently. For the company's growth, conflicts, whether positive or negative, need to be addressed immediately.

Effects of Unresolved Conflict in a Workplace

"Complaining about a problem without posing a solution is called whining."

— Teddy Roosevelt

Conflicts in the workplace are like a terminal illness that does not surface immediately but can be averted if detected early. Conflict can permeate all areas of the organization and thus affect employees, customers, and stakeholders. Hence, organizations need to adopt mechanisms for early detection and solution of the conflict in the workplace.

Employees also have a significant role to play when there is negative conflict in the organization; they need to know how to read the situation, quell tensions, and manage conflicts. You can't see a fire and walk right into it. So, it is imperative to train employees to resolve minor issues among themselves rather than call on the organization's leadership to intervene and mediate each time there is a problem. It is wiser for organizational leaders to have all-hands-on-deck when developing conflict resolution mechanisms. Apart from the fact that it helps the employees learn better ways to manage conflicts, it also gives them a sense of belonging. However, neglect of issues that may lead to conflict connotes that the leaders are not committed to the organization's human capital development, and besides that, your organization will be on the path to losing money. One of the instabilities that will arise from conflict is that employees will become detached from their original ideal. There can be deliberate sabotage of other team members' efforts, which may affect the entire organization. Unresolved conflict is a detrimental factor that robs an organization of all its hard work. For example, suppose there is an unresolved conflict. In that case, the unmotivated employee will start showing signs of incompetence; some employees may miss deadlines and affect productivity. These factors can hinder the organization's progress because the employees arc not performing their duties as they should. It can also affect the other departments within the organization. This says a lot about the losses that the company will record if drastic steps are not taken to resolve whatever conflicts may be present.

Toxic Workplace Environment

Many people may not be aware that health-related illnesses can stem from an organization and employees. In many health literature readings, you will find lots of information about how illnesses can be triggered by increased stress levels that affect the immune system and weaken the body's resistance to diseases. Emotional conflict can create a lot of stress in individuals. When the pressure becomes frequent, it can have a detrimental effect on employees' health. Due to my desire to become an expert in Alternative Dispute Resolution (ADR), which can also be referred to as the Conflict Resolution field, I have had my fair share of health issues as a result of the toxicity of some workplaces, which I will share further in this book. Many organizational leaders are blind to how much it costs the company's reputation and productivity when conflicts are not resolved.

Many organizational leaders also think that human conflict is nipped in the bud or managed with the interference of the typical Human Resource professionals. However, many of them do not know how to deal with human conflict. They often implement the carrot and stick principle to contain or eradicate the organization's human conflict. This is an obsolete approach that could escalate the conflict rather than deescalate it as expected. Look at the curriculum throughout many Human Resource university-level degrees, as well as professional certifications. You will discover that the curriculum rarely includes conflict resolution skills. I know this because when I pursued a related certification through the University of California, Santa Cruz Extension in Silicon Valley in 2020, I was invited an instructor to teach conflict resolution courses, mediation, diversity, and inclusion (another subject Human Resource does not cover in the education curriculum).

If Human Resource professionals take the initiative and pick some insightful information from here to add to their toolbox of skills, they will become better at conflict resolution. Unfortunately, the rigidity of following policies and procedures in their organization takes precedence, rather than looking at resolving the conflict with empathy. Besides this fact, you have corporate legal counsel that directs Human Resources to manage employees' conflict based on a narrow-tunnel- vision that follows legalities to protect the company's image. My intent here is to open the organizational leaders' eyes to realizing that the human resource's methodology for resolving conflicts is not working.

The world is evolving fast, and humans are becoming more aware of their environments, stressors, and flawed principles that guide their activities as employees, among other factors affecting their lives. The internet has made it easier for people to share information and resources. So, employees from different organizations can interact with each other and get information on the type of treatment they get in the various companies. At the moment, a lot of people are not looking to just work because they need to. Instead, they are looking to work in places where they can happily perform their duties with minimal stress and conflicts. The Industrial Revolution gave birth to various management theories and concepts, many of which are still used in today's workforce. However, it is essential to note that most of these theories are obsolete and may not be effective today. The workforce has evolved with the adoption of technological innovations and systems.

My Personal Story in A Toxic Work Environment

Please know that this is the first time I share this personal story about my experience with a toxic workplace environment, so you are privileged to read this first-hand from me. I kept it quiet for many years as I was still working for the same educational institution. I needed to be careful what I shared with anyone about the institution. In 2008, I decided to pursue a master's degree. While researching the available courses I could pick, I found one that caught my attention in "Negotiation, Conflict Resolution, and Peace-building."

It was love at first sight when I read about this unique degree, and it was precisely the skills I felt I needed instead of getting an MBA. I started my master's degree in this area and simultaneously enrolled in obtaining a year-long certification in leadership coaching. When I started my first educational semester, I had to transition to a different department at the university I was working for because the funding for the program I worked for was running low. That was due to the economic recession, which caused a reduction in funding. As I always say, be careful what you ask the universe for because you do not know how it may manifest and affect your life. I was so passionate about my education that I committed to learning everything that would help me become an expert in the field. Still, I never expected that I would be enrolling in a PhD. at an experiential level in my workplace while studying for my master's degree and my coaching credential.

As kind and naïve as I was, I transitioned to a department under one of the Dean of the university I worked. The Dean was around my age, if not a few years older, and I was his assistant. Believe it or not, I had never heard or knew anything that had to do with workplace bullying, micromanagement, and cliques at work. Guess what? I got to personally experience all these three behaviors in that department. The department staff did not trust me because I worked directly with the Dean. Therefore, I was excluded from the group for any department meetings, decisions, lunches, and co-worker's get-together.

Besides not feeling a sense of belonging, my boss was always breathing down my neck. He micromanaged every assignment I had to do for him and requested that I not talk to other employees in my department. Furthermore, there was a continuous check to ensure that I was at my desk whenever my hour lunch ended. My empathy, resilience, knowledge about human behavior, and emotional intelligence, especially my coaching education, helped me better manage the situation. It helped me understand the motives behind the behavior of my boss and those of my co-workers. Imagine this; I had been a single mom dealing with a problematic teenager at home. I was also dealing with health issues for a few years before starting to work with the Dean. Still, none of these situations prevented me from ever being present at my job. I enjoyed working with students at the university and loved my office setting with a nice window overseeing the entire college campus.

It took about two years of dealing with the toxic work environment before realizing the stress was getting to me psychologically and physically. One day I woke up and realized that I couldn't get up from my bed because the right side of my body was numb. Friends took me to the hospital, and all they could say was that it was the stress I was dealing with at work that had done that to my body. Months before this happened to me, I had already been seeking psychological therapy from therapists for support. I noticed that my workplace environment was the precursor of my post-traumatic stress disorders and severe heart palpitations. My therapists had to force me into short-term disability, with me kicking and screaming that I could not afford to do that. Also, I didn't want to have the stigma of being seen as a bad employee. I had no idea that the short-term disability was part of my workplace benefit. Right after I started my short-term disability, I received a call from the Human Resource department where I answered several questions about what had happened to me, why I never reported the abuse to HR, and how they wanted me to document all that had happened.

Later I learned that the Human Resource department was not necessarily worried about me; rather, they were looking for more evidence against the Dean because I wasn't the first person who had gotten into some health issue due to the toxic environment. He had already sent three professors into workers compensation disability, a very different disability benefit only used for employees who had suffered an injury or illness at work. Well, I never got that option; instead, they left me to suffer economic consequences as the short-term disability was less than half of my monthly earnings. This experience is how I learned first-hand what can happen to a person when dealing with a toxic workplace environment. If someone had told me before my personal experience that your health could deteriorate drastically because of a toxic workplace environment, I would never have believed it.

A lot has been done recently by several state legislators throughout the United States to create awareness about the health dangers to employees when working in hostile workplace conditions. In 2015, legislators throughout different states, including California, adopted new legislation to add to the already required yearly sexual harassment training, an integral part of workplace harassment. Unfortunately, it is not as effective as it should be because workplace harassment is only illegal if the perpetrator or bully is directing the harassment to what Human Resource called protected categories, including persons of a different race, people over 40 years of age, religion, or sexual orientation.

The Value of Positive Culture in Organizations

Numerous research studies have demonstrated that one of the most sought-after skills in the workforce is dealing with or managing workplace human conflict. The Association for Talent and Development (ATD) commented in their 2019 research report titled "The Future of Work: Technology, Predictions, and Preparing the Workforce" that conflict resolution skills are some of the essential skills necessary in today's workforce. According to Eugene Kogan of the Harvard Division of Continuing Education, in his 2020 blog post, 3 Effective Strategies to Manage Workplace Conflict, he pointed out that conflict resolution is a crucial element in improving the dynamics for yourself and your team. By employing conflict resolution strategies, people can transcend the immediate tension and move the relationship to a more productive stage.

Positive culture emanates from effective communication in the workplace. One of the few ways to reduce conflict in the workplace is to communicate your feelings appropriately. This culture goes beyond just making your point known but understanding where the other person is coming from as well. It is essential to be empathetic in resolving a conflict. You can show empathy by being a good listener. Communication, therefore, cannot be complete without appropriate feedback. Employees need to strive to communicate without being condescending or rude towards the other party to buy respect while sharing the issues between them.

3

People Skills Are Not Soft Skills

> *"What Got You Here Won't Get You There."*
>
> —*Dr. Marshall Goldsmith*

The leaky bottom line of the organization explains how conflict hampers the revenue and finances of an organization. As such, leaders need skills that can help revive their finances and other areas of the organization. This chapter seeks to show the essence of having excellent soft and hard skills.

The way you treat people stems from the kind of interaction you have with them. Human relationships focus on fostering personal and close ties with people with whom you share a common goal, interest, values, and beliefs. When you think about it in a broader sense, humans move by the same shared plan; live and prosper. The need to be fair and interact with people regardless of social status, religion, background, and age makes it easy for human relationships to thrive. Good interpersonal relationships with fellow humans are one way of unlocking doors of possibilities in different areas of people's life. As earlier explained, no human is an island; establishing excellent and meaningful relationships in various spheres of our lives helps us become better.

Organizations still have a long way to go before realizing the importance of fostering good interpersonal relationships between leaders and employees. The essence of interpersonal relationships in organizations goes beyond the normal communication flow among employees. Still, it is also crucial among departments to impact good productivity and the overall success of organizations. Consequently, hiring people with excellent interpersonal skills is critical, especially when dynamism is the order for businesses in today's world. The acquisition of relevant technical or hard skills for a person to be employable in the workforce is no longer enough. Skilled workers must gain interpersonal skills or what is called "People's Skills." For instance, Jim is proficient in hard skills such as copywriting, content marketing, and graphic design, making him an essential person in the organization's makeup. However, Jim has poor interpersonal skills, his problem being not knowing how to communicate effectively with fellow team members, thereby hampering productivity regardless of his expertise. In retrospect, without effective communication, organizations cannot achieve their goals. Human interaction is the oil that keeps the engine running in organizations. This chapter will show the need to equip our workforce with good soft skills needed to enter the workplace and enhance the organization's brand image and profits.

What are Soft Skills?

Soft skills or people skills are those skills that people learn through their interactions with other humans. Soft skills are shown through personal traits, characters, and values that influence how individuals work with each other. Soft skills are necessary ingredients for creating a smooth, positive, and productive work environment in any organization.

Many organizations still focus on hiring people for their hard skills and overlooking whether they have soft skills or not. There is a famous quote from Dr. Marshall Goldsmith, who I had the pleasure to be invited to his home in San Diego, California, back in 2016. The quote reads, "What got you here won't get you there," from one of his best-selling books, "What Got You Here Won't Get You There: How Successful People Become Even More Successful." In this book, he explained that he had coached most leader's regarding people's skills in his many years of coaching Fortune 500 leaders in Silicon Valley and worldwide. He explains that it is typical for an organization to hire leaders who know the organization's ins and outs and have university-level degrees. Yet, these same leaders either become stagnated or get in trouble in their career ladder ascension when they do not know how to lead people and resolve conflicts among employees in the organization.

What is worse is that everyone in the organization assumes that they know how to manage workplace conflict because they are in a leadership role. Still, the reality is that most of them are not skilled in these essential people skills, just as we see in the Human Resource department. When hiring staff, it is best to go for good people skills as an added advantage. Another thing to note; to cope with the ever-changing business world, people who may not have the same experience of a job role as others within an organization, but have amazing soft skills, tend to thrive and perform better in the workplace because people like to work with other people that they like and can easily get along with.

The workplace and workforce experienced a paradigm shift

when COVID-19 hit, and a lot of organizations had to adopt remote operations. Employees still need soft skills to work effectively, even when working remotely. Sure, people work from the comfort of their homes, but the ability to interact and get valuable information from coworkers takes soft skills. We have technology to thank for ensuring work continues regardless of the horrid times the world is facing.

Technology has made work a bit more seamless, and that is why you can now work from the comfort of your homes, with all the necessary applications and utilities you need to get the job done effectively and efficiently. The global pandemic has dramatically increased the popularity of remote jobs in the United States, where sectors like education, food and hospitality, sports, and others have been able to cope during the difficult times caused by the pandemic. At this moment, we need interpersonal relationships more than ever because your success and productivity from working remotely somewhat rely on how good your relationship is with your colleagues. If you need something, you could easily text your colleagues and get favorable responses, especially if it is time-based; however, their answer is dependent on how good your relationship is with them. If you do not have good relationships with some of your colleagues, they might well see your messages, texts, emails and still ignore them.

List of Soft skills

Here are some soft skills that should be high on the list of priorities that organizations should consider when hiring candidates:
- Emotional Intelligence,
- Conflict resolution,
- Integrity,
- Effective communication,

- Creativity,
- Teamwork,
- Critical thinking,
- Empathy,
- Resilience,
- Growth Mindset,
- Adaptability.

Employees that operate above the egocentric level of consciousness adopt these skills with ease and successfully implement them. However, the implementation of these skills varies as there are different levels of consciousness that each individual may have been able to master. It is possible for employees and leaders to have one or more of these skill sets but never to the same degree.

The combination of hard skills and soft skills in any workplace is sure to enhance productivity at all levels. Imagine if more than 70% of people had excellent hard and soft skills in your organization, work will be made easier, employees will achieve set objectives, and advancement in career will be the norm.

The Lack of Conflict Resolution in The Workplace Today

Most organizations make life a bit difficult for employees with the kind of treatment they receive. As such, there is no impetus to resolve any conflict. Suppose we could solve problems and achieve an organization's set goals on our own. In that case, there won't be any need for meetings, brainstorming sessions, and collaborative efforts.

It is important to note that an individual can be knowledgeable about the educational side of things or acquire hard skills such as data analysis but have difficulty working collaboratively with other people. This point stems from a host of factors: students do not learn soft skills in schools, as they are not really taught in elementary, middle school, high school, college, or university. Although some school curriculum centers on leadership and development skills, most of what students learn revolves around principles and theories. To correct the issues currently faced by this generation, schools need to implement several programs that foster all students' participation in presenting ideas for a particular project.

As much as the inclusion of soft skill courses is important in schools, most of the strategies we use to resolve conflicts originate from social interaction. The evidence of different social groups in schools transcends to the latter parts of our lives as people tend to identify with a group that best suits them. Employees who have issues relating to people have always had that problem while growing up; the evolution of social interaction results from their encounters. We tend to resolve issues based on our exposure to different conflict resolution techniques garnered from parents, friends, school, religion, marriage, politics, television, and other areas of our lives. Through our exposure to learning from other conflict resolution skills, we pick up soft skills. Unfortunately, we do not have outstanding role models in society that we can imitate good soft skills. It all takes you to turn on your TV to see many shows that sell good ratings by showing people fighting with each other and negatively competing with each other. If you pay attention, our current politicians are enacting fights against one another all the time, as if it was an extension of their high school popularity contest and drama. Wrong role models in society have possibly contributed to some employees' low conflict resolution techniques.

The Issue of Technology

> *"I fear the day that technology will surpass our human interaction. The world will have a generation of idiots."*
>
> *—Albert Einstein*

Sadly, Einstein's quote has come to play in present times. Technology has brought a lot of joy to the world but also indulged a lot of lonely people by lessening interactions with others. The ease through which systems function in the world is made possible through technological advancement. However, the younger generations have become overly engrossed with their phones, laptops, and other gadgets. Thus, building strong and meaningful bonds with other people has become a difficult thing to do. Of course, there will be increased use of smartphones as our health, banking, friends, food, and lives are attached to the mobility of our actions and interactions. Our dependence on these mobile devices for getting certain tasks done cannot be downplayed; however, where physical interactions with other people come into view, we seem to be more focused on these devices than having honest conversations with people. Families now have dinners without saying a word to each other; couples lay next to each other on the bed but are total strangers every night. They are more engrossed in the social media happenings on their smartphones than paying attention to each other. Technology has made people heavily dependent on gadgets. It is getting so bad that it has become difficult for people to put down their phones and have actual conversations with those around them.

The inability to properly communicate with other people hinders the effectiveness of the work done in an organization.

Lack of healthy interpersonal relationships can cause issues to an individual's mental and physical well-being, but what is the benefit of having an employee who delivers on time but does not have any friends? Eventually, the sadness will overwhelm the employee, causing a meltdown that could be harmful to others. In essence, capitalizing on the advantages of technology affords us the luxury to solidify our existing relationships and establish new ones. Technology makes provisions for developing good human relationships with people even outside your country. Social media allows individuals to reach millions of people; there are online groups and forums to find people with similar likes and beliefs.

When a healthy workplace environment is established, there is more fluidity in the organization, as people exchange ideas. Those who have issues meet people who can solve them, and there is a higher level of trust when ideas are shared. Effective communication eases tension in the workplace, and sometimes, all you have to do is have a one-on-one with the person to bring clarity.

PEOPLE SKILLS ARE NOT SOFT SKILLS

4

What Our Ancestors Can Teach Us

> *"I believe that what we become depends on what our fathers teach us at odd moments when they aren't trying to teach us. Little scraps of wisdom form us."*
>
> —*Umberto Eco*

Without having the right skills, we would not be able to follow in the footsteps of our ancestors. The skills are necessary for establishing relationships with members of the organization. You will be able to see how these skills help in an organization and interact with colleagues.

If there is anything COVID-19 has taught us, it is that changes can happen at any time. We saw how the COVID-19 pandemic affected every industry and sector in different parts of the world and caused a downturn in the world economy. As a result of the tragedy, many people lost their jobs, and in a bid to keep their businesses afloat, organizations had to terminate people's contracts considering there was not enough inflow. Putting the tension experienced by everyone in every part of the world does not do justice to what people went through. Even at the time of writing this book, several other companies were downsizing to stay relevant in business.

Moreover, it has created a certain level of instability, fear, and conflict within the organizations. No one wants to make a mistake; at this point, no error is excusable. Interestingly, some people in specific organizations are living on borrowed time, juggling between not failing at work to not dying from a deadly virus on your way to work. The pandemic made it difficult for people to visit friends and family, and many employees in different parts of the world had to learn to cope with these circumstances. While employees may have different issues to deal with, especially when a pandemic is involved, organizations are not left out of the troubled waters. This is why many businesses are not as vibrant as they used to be. For instance, an immigration firm that helps process visas for clients to other countries could not comfortably pay their staff due to the travel restrictions. The pandemic made it very difficult for many businesses to function normally. Everyone had to look for ways to adapt to the new normal, which included downsizing and asking employees to work remotely. Therefore, issues centered on diversity, equality, inclusion, and equal employment opportunities became critical areas that organizations had to deal with. Organizations must have a system where employees can speak freely about irregularities and how they affect them, giving employees the freedom to share their personal opinions, suggestions and proffer solutions. ADR, which is an acronym for Alternative Dispute Resolution, is a strategy that promotes practices that help to resolve conflicts in a non-threatening and approachable way. Organizations employ

ADR professionals that help navigate the organization's issues and uncover the most critical factors that contribute to harmful disputes in the workplace.

The Power of Talking It Out

Talking things out is very therapeutic because you can air your grievances and enjoy some relief from the process. Organizations need a system where employees can voice their issues, opinions and even suggest ideas to their team leads. It is important to note that a free flow of exchange of ideas between leaders and employees makes the team a better unit. Also, in talking things out with the team lead, the employees might put some great ideas forward. As a team leader, giving credit to the employee responsible for a brilliant idea provides room for more creative thinking, and it also provides the employee with a sense of belonging to the group. Employees who are not good with group discussions can go privately to meet with the leader to resolve conflicts that may hinder their productivity and progress.

The power of talking things out is as old as human existence, considering that the first step at resolving conflicts was by talking about them. In essence, talking is the early stage of getting to the root of an organization's problems – you should never assume because it is common knowledge that assumption is the enemy of progress. If you conduct adequate research by asking questions, conflict resolution comes more effectively.

Consequently, finding time to meet with employees as the team leader is imperative. Sometimes making the first move might just save the organization a whole lot of money. Some employees might be timid to go to their supervisor or manager to discuss what is bothering them. Still, a casual stroll around the building and randomly talking to staff helps the leader get more information about what is going on in the organization. In a bid to address a larger number of people to help resolve conflict before it escalates, here are some of our ancestor's strategies we can use today.

Dialogue Circles

A smart person knows what to say. A wise person knows whether to say it or not."

— *Anonymous*

In the times where communal living was the only kind of residential arrangement, men and women representing their different households would gather in a circle to discuss ways to move the community forward. It is a facilitation exercise that allowed people to speak freely without any reproach or degradation about their class or way of life. Fast forward many years later, and we, as a global village, have adopted this form of conflict resolution technique to talk about the issues plaguing the organization collectively.

So here is how it works in modern times:

The CEO calls for a meeting with every employee and subordinate head. It could be a day at the office or a particular day from work. Either way, every organization member needs to be present to make decision-making faster and resolve the conflicts more profoundly. However, opting for a day separate from the regular working hours is best as there is a relaxed environment when the employees are not bothered about the work they have suspended for the meeting. A plan will guide the meeting course to prevent rambling on without making any headway.

Consequently, everybody is given an equal opportunity to talk about different matters, no matter how small or insignificant it may seem. Encouraging people to talk will help get diverse opinions about how best to tackle issues and resolve conflicts. As a result of the pandemic, technology has become an important part of these meetings, as they can be carried out remotely. Thus, it removes the nervousness that some people may experience if they were meeting physically.

Dialogue Circles to promote Diversity, Equity, and Inclusion (DEI) in organizations

As long as there is a gathering of humans, every organization has some degree of diversity, whether in language, orientation, style, and other peculiarities and as such, employees need, now more than ever, conversations centered on DEI to avoid any form of negative bias in the workplace. Therefore, DEI is a susceptible subject that people need to discuss more often to prevent massive workplace conflicts. Equal opportunity employers help promote diversity, equity, and inclusion among the employees. Such organizations need to show that all benefits, compensations, and benefits of working there would be available to all employees. DEI reforms in the workplace need the organization's attention to avoid conflicts that can escalate into tarnishing the organization's reputation. If correctly planned and executed, DEI helps reshape the organization to include all employees in the system. When every member, regardless of nationality, language, or heritage, feels included, there is increased productivity. If the dialogue includes everyone, then there will be greater participation in the scheme of things.

The clamor for a DEI facilitator who understands the left-out employees' pain is also critical in this discussion. The facilitator's prerogative is to promote an arena where all employees have equal opportunities just as any other person in the organization, regardless of their race; the employees are eligible for promotion, a raise, and other benefits that come with working for the organization. In the previous chapter, we talked about the factors that contribute to conflicts in the workplace. One of those factors was poor working conditions. The negligence by the organization of adding every member to the promotion list makes it very hard for people to thrive in that organization. If an organization fails to include every team member in daily affairs, the consequences might be severe, taking us back to the leaky bottom-line.

Gaining conflict intelligence is a two-way street as it requires both the organization leaders' and the employees' participation. On the organization's path, the team leaders should create an ambiance conducive to the employees' learning, growth, and productivity. It helps to improve the quality of life and mitigates risks of conflicts by ensuring an all-inclusive environment for all races, ethnicities, and gender to fully function and become a more significant part of the organization. It can mean creating a better work schedule that makes work equal for employees and the metrics for promotion accessible to all organization members.

The leaders need to transcend from levels of consciousness that are egocentric and mundane. The realization that life is worth more will help them provide a better working environment for employees to thrive. The same goes for the need for employees to see themselves as a part of an organization; making a difference will mitigate conflict. If employees see themselves as part of an organization's future, there is a high tendency not to need any form of extra motivation to get work done. There will also be room for sharing ideas and expanding the horizons of creativity through brainstorming sessions, debates, dialogue circles, and other meetings to help strategize new ways to move the organization to the next level.

Furthermore, accepting faults and seeking correction comes with a mature group of consciousness which both leaders and employees can inculcate. As human beings, we are flawed because we do not always have all the right answers. Therefore, leaders need to create a warm atmosphere where employees can share ideas and talk about the unit's issues, and the organization alone can reduce conflicts. Leaders can learn from employees and vice versa; understanding each other is essential in ensuring the work environment's peace and tranquility.

Finally, we all are human beings before we belong to any group, nationality, or tribe. As a result of this, treating others the same way you will treat yourself is the best principle in avoiding conflicts in the workplace and life. Yes! Conflicts will come because of the disparity in our evolution as adults but resolving them takes us seeing humanity first before anything else.

5

What is Conflict Intelligence Quotient (Conflict-IQ)™ ?

> *"The most profound personal growth does not happen while reading a book or meditating on a mat. It happens in the throes of conflict - when you are angry, afraid, frustrated. It happens when you are doing the same old thing and you suddenly realize that you have a choice."*
>
> —Vironika Tugaleva

This chapter opens us to the adoption of Conflict Intelligence Quotient "Conflict-IQ™" as a needed trait for leaders and employees. The ability to deal with diverse and multicultural people in an organization will be examined here.

As a child, I always admired how my father could build trust in his employees, which inspired me to become an avid learner of leadership development. In the past nine years, thanks to all my clients I had the privilege to work with, I developed my conflict management skills. As I worked with clients; some with very high levels of education, and others self-made, I was intrigued to realize that it was not their intelligence that helped them deal with human conflict, nor was it their degrees that determined how well they could deal with interpersonal or intrapersonal issues; or made them advance in their careers as leaders in their organizations, but their abilities to employ the proper conflict management techniques at the right time.

I had a client, let's call him Pedro, from whom I learned the most and who helped me realize how I contributed to the leadership development of the people around me. Pedro was a young man who did not have any formal education. He came from a migrant family that had no affluence. He worked in a restaurant and was developing his small business on the side. Pedro came to me because he wanted to get coaching on how to advance in his small business. The young man had problems having difficult conversations with one of his business partners. Coaching him made it very clear that he possessed a resiliency that he gained through his life, and it helped him become a small company leader. He also felt that he was not intelligent because he remembered that as a child, he compared himself to others in the classroom and concluded that he was not smart. Furthermore, he also shared with me that those same students he used to compare himself with, although they were intelligent, they had not been able to achieve as much as he had in life. He had an "Aha" moment when I explained to him the distinction between intelligence (IQ) and emotional intelligence (EQ).

IQ = is used to determine mental and academic abilities.
EQ = is defined as an individual's ability to identify, evaluate, control, and express emotions.

Pedro was able to discern from IQ and EQ, and his self-esteem started to build. He realized that his disposition to experience and learn from life had got him to where he was in his life. The young man moved to the United States at the age of 15, all by himself. He traveled to different places around the United States until he felt it was the right place to start his business. He began by getting and holding on to a job that would support him and help him achieve his dream of becoming an entrepreneur. I think what inspired me the most was that, in some way, he reminded me so much of my father's story. I had the opportunity to help Pedro become more aware of his emotional intelligence. I also helped him get to a level where he felt confident to deal with the human conflict that he was experiencing with his business partner. He gained Conflict Intelligence; Conflict-IQ™ .

Conflict Intelligence "Conflict-IQ™" is a way of recognizing, comprehending, and making conscious choices on how to handle emotions, ways of thinking, and behaviors amid dealing with an intrapersonal (within individual mind or self) and interpersonal (involving relationship between others) conflict.

The ability to become a Conflict-IQ™ individual allows you to raise your consciousness levels. This state will enable you to shape your interactions with others and understand your inner-self, tendencies, and abilities to make thoughtful choices rather than reacting to a circumstance amid emotions or reactions that you might regret later.

My dedication to the field of Alternative Dispute Resolution (ADR) is not only subject to my attaining a master-level education in this field, but I also got more knowledge from reading every single book on the subject that I came across. I also loved attending endless hours of training and gaining certification in each area of this field.

FIGURE 2

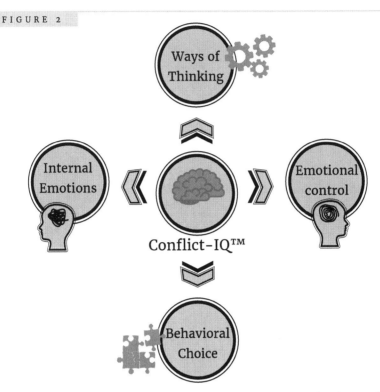

Conflict-IQ™

Also, I gained knowledge from any mentors who had paved the way in this field and taught university-level institution courses, and volunteering in numerous organizations. I volunteered as a conflict resolution specialist, mediator, and coach to discover how to lead others through the Unitive Way of achieving Conflict Intelligence.

Conflict Intelligence's foundation comes first and foremost by gaining awareness, awareness of your feelings, and understanding your history. You see, our educational institutions do not teach us or skill us in this essential people skill. Now more and more, some universities are starting to add a course in this subject in their MBA program, and there are some certifications here and there that you can attain through some university extension programs. Dealing with human conflict is part of life;

how did we miss people on this critical skill? Have you ever heard friends refer to workplace conflict as feeling like they are back in middle school? In some parts, this is very true because we go on in life thinking that we are gaining enough knowledge and skill that will eventually help us be successful in the workplace from our educational institutions. The reality is that there are minimal jobs where people do not work with other people. Whenever we have more than one employee or person involved, there is a set of ideas, values, beliefs, tendencies, personality styles that will always be different from anyone else. I have never heard that there is one brain similar to another brain, have you?

What do people do when they face a situation where they feel threatened, attacked, or feel like they do not agree on things with others or even themselves? They go to their mental archives of the past and bring outdated conflict resolution skills that they learned as they were growing up. Very few people take the initiative or responsibility to go out of their way to learn new ways on how to deal with their conflict and that with others.

Unfortunately, many of us did not have good role models that taught us civil ways to deal with conflicts in our life. We live in a society that rewards us through damaging competitiveness, fights, drama, revenge, and gaining the upper hand on others. Many of us grow up watching aggressive sports, violent movies, trashy reality shows, and entertaining programs showing dehumanized fighting. We do not have many places where we can imitate constructive, good civil behavior to deal with human conflict.

The next step is to unlearn the negative behavioral programming that you have had throughout your life. Once we have a clean slate, we start with the new programming. The good thing is that neuroscience teaches us that our brains can learn and unlearn at any age of our life. That is what scientists call neuroplasticity - helping the brain change through growth and the reorganization of information.

Neuroplasticity = the ability of the brain to form and reorganize synaptic connections, mostly in response to learning or experience or following injury. It can also be referred to as rewiring the brain.

When experiencing conflict as a disruption in our relationships' natural flow, we cannot stop and notice something is not right. Our minds tend to focus more on things we did not notice when the relationship was going smoothly. Our mind takes more energy to interpret and re-interpret what things mean and what happened during a conflict. Our mind goes into a state of fight-or-flight, fear, and stress. Our communication will be more difficult, taking more effort. Our physiology changes as our feelings translate from uneasiness to anxiety or even outright pain. When there is a conflict, we have opportunities to see things from a different perspective. Thus, they transform it from an emotional conflict, which can be irrational and escalate quickly to a cognitive conflict, rationally de-escalating the situation and reaching a more peaceful resolution.

It is when we gain perception to see the conflict from a different perspective that we can recognize:

- The actual immediate situation,
- Underlying patterns and context,
- A conceptual framework of what is happening,
- See the conflict as regular and dynamic within human relationships,
- Envision conflict positively as a natural phenomenon that creates a potential for positive growth,
- Conflict to have the possibility of a constructive change.

It is my highest desire to get as many people as possible to understand that conflict can move from being a destructive pattern to being constructive. It only takes YOU to make such a difference. Of course, some instruction is required to do so.

The Role of Emotional Intelligence in Conflict Resolution

The evolution of workplace culture has seen emotional intelligence and conflict management take center stage. Studies around emotional intelligence have peaked since the last decade. Scholars have uncovered the discourse being the instigator for behavior in an organization. The history of emotional intelligence can be traced to two psychologists who viewed the subject as a way of gazing through one's feelings, thoughts, and emotions to guide one's actions in a complex environment such as we find ourselves today. Understanding the way people think and perceive situations is imperative in resolving conflict in an organization. Emotional intelligence is not just for leaders in a workplace but also for employees who continually collaborate with other people to actualize their goals and objectives. Emotional intelligence involves the subtle reading of cues, whether non-verbal or verbal cues, to know what to do and when to speak. For employees, being emotionally intelligent means the ability to recognize the best time to speak and act after considering all the relevant factors.

Scholars believe that two models make up emotional intelligence. These elements come to play in different situations in an organization. These models are:

The mental ability: This relates to the emotions of the employee or person.

The mixed model explains the intellectual process – the

combination of mental and non-mental abilities, according to Myer et al. (2000).

We will use these models to explain the essence of emotional intelligence in conflict resolution. The mental ability has some dimensions which are arranged from the smallest to the most complex. Each area has a particular role to play and is used by leaders and employees trained in conflict management.

Perceiving and expressing entails employees' and leaders' ability to recognize their emotions and feelings while considering other people's thoughts. This will help ensure effective communication, and there is a shared understanding of where both parties stand. Emotional intelligence allows employees and leaders to understand the way other people feel. It gives an inclination to what the person is going through at that particular time.

Assimilating emotions in thought is the second dimension that explains the mental ability of emotionally intelligent people. This allows people to facilitate different changes in their thinking, actions, and behavior. Emotional intelligence is very strategic and has to be employed by people who understand these models. The dimension explains that by understanding the employee's needs, feelings, and grievances, the other party can change and act differently. In essence, emotional intelligence is the trait that allows people to act differently.

Understanding emotions is the third dimension that speaks of employees understanding the root causes of the behavior. Emotionally intelligent people do not stop looking at the surface but dig deep in understanding why they react in such a manner. Emotional intelligence helps uncover profound truths and mysteries that have affected the individual or the workplace as a whole. It may be that the issue is the leaders always shy away from intervening in matters; hence, this nature has become part of the organization. Therefore, there would be a lot of unresolved cases adding to the tension in the organization.

Depending on the context, emotional intelligence gives people the ability to manage their emotions. No conflict is resolved in the same way. You can take the ideas from past experiences, but you may need to invent new ways since the workplace is dynamic. Therefore, managing emotions could mean taking a break from the heated area and meditating, which is discussed in-depth in future chapters.

The mixed ability makes up for the second part of emotional intelligence. It shows the intellectual process and how they interact with emotions. Self-awareness is a critical element of emotional intelligence; we will discuss it more in-depth in subsequent chapters. Emotionally intelligent people are always conscious of both environment and the other parties. The environment consists of all things that make up the emotional, physical, cultural, and social components of that person. Emotional intelligence is the tool that many people use to communicate effectively without shades of prejudice and discrimination.

Emotional intelligence does not just help in conflict management but also allows employees of diverse cultures, sex, age, and status to cohabit. Relationships are built based on ample emotional intelligence in the organization. Therefore, without equipping the leaders and employees with dynamic intelligence tools, it will be impossible to achieve productivity. Emotional intelligence can't be overemphasized as more dynamism is apparent in today's culture with people representing different communities in organizations.

6

Conflict Intelligence Methods

"The most difficult thing in any negotiation, almost, is making sure that you strip it of the emotion and deal with the facts."

—*Howard Baker*

This chapter continues to explore the intricacies of conflict intelligence as an essential discourse in an organization's growth. Here, we will see how to implement the methods that increase conflict intelligence in leaders and employees.

We must understand our upbringings, the environment we were raised in and comprehend that we are in this together. Not many of us have ever stopped to think about how we deal with conflict and make a conscious effort to learn different ways of gaining tools to become more conflict competent. Human beings don't change behaviors or learn anything until it costs them money, severe pain, or gain gratification. This is why I focus on teaching professionals how to apply Conflict-IQ™ methodologies because their biggest motivator is when their career is on the line. My undercover motive is that I like to work with motivated professionals. They end up realizing that applying Conflict-IQ™ benefits not only their professional life but also their personal life. I hope that our workplace professionals become better employees and help companies become better family members, better friends, better community citizens, and overall better human beings for humanity's global benefit. I know I am a dreamer, but Disneyland also started with a dream, right?

This is how my mind engineered the creation of what I like to call the Conflict-IQ™ methodology. I firmly believe that learning the Conflict-IQ™ methodology will augment people's emotional intelligence and help them become better humans.

Self-Awareness

Conflict-IQ™ includes the development of fundamental emotional factors, which in turn have numerous sub-factors. Self-awareness is critical in the unfolding process of understanding the problematic aspect of every person. To start the process is to identify your personality style and the way you deal with human conflict. There are many personality style assessments that you can use to understand your tendencies. You can check to see which personality style assessments your organization already has in place by asking your Human Resource Department or your Talent and Development Department.

Self-Awareness is also essential when it comes to identifying your conflict styles. In 1974, Kenneth W. Thomas and Ralph H. Kilmann introduced a beneficial conflict mode instrument. It helped identify conflict styles from the assertiveness or cooperativeness spectrum. Once you understand the preliminary conflict style that you execute naturally, you can start learning to liberate yourself from that predominant behavioral pattern to strategically select the most appropriate spectrum depending on the actual conflict and the environment where this conflict has enacted the importance level.

Another area where it is crucial to create self-awareness is in the area of triggers. What is it that alters your emotions, feelings, and behaviors either unconsciously or consciously? Identifying your triggers is imperative. Some triggers could come from people, a particular tone of voice, particular behaviors, people's ways of being, values, and beliefs. These triggers are essential in learning how to remove the emotional or behavioral effect on yourself from other people's communication methods. This communication from another human being can come into your brain through all your human senses (visual, kinesthetic, auditory, smell). We also have a sense of intuition. Your brain is an archive of memories. Our mind can become triggered to a fast emotional or thought reaction when anyone does something that reminds us of a negative experience. You might not know why you are reacting to someone or something they did in many instances. You must start paying attention to the triggers and start analyzing them to remove the effects they have on you.

Understanding yourself and your tendencies when conflict arises internally or manifests between and other people will allow you to be more aware of your emotional state.

Re-Tooling the Brain, Reactions, and Behavior

In my experience, while working with so many clients, it can be challenging to try to install conflict resolution tools or methodology if self-awareness does not happen first. Once a person has the space capacity in their mind when working on self-awareness, it is easier to help install information useful when experiencing Intra/inter conflict. Gaining new knowledge, understanding the practical skills that come with every single personality trait, inner awareness, and outer awareness of behaviors of others and your reactions is a necessary process.

It is also essential to apply a methodology to resolve or manage a conflict and deliver this in an experiential process. There are many conflict resolution online training programs that are cookie-cutters and do not make a dent in people's minds or abilities to resolve conflict. Teaching conflict resolution skills requires experience and practice in a safe setting where the teacher feels competent and comfortable using real-world lessons.

Also, people have to learn based on a relationship-centered approach. This means that conflict resolution or conflict management is not only to reach agreement and solution, but instead, that the teaching promotes constructive change processes inclusive of, but not limited to, immediate solution. To envision a present problem in the eye of opportunity within which relationships are essential in resolving or managing a conflict.

It is also essential to install within these tools how to map the situation. When conflict becomes visible to the people involved in it and to the others observing it or sensing it, it gets attention. Insidious conflict often starts as something minor, way before it manifests into something visible. Many times, people are not aware or remember when it started.

In today's busy and often chaotic world, people get caught in the trap of working on tasks instead of working with people because it is easier to work on things than with people, mainly when they cannot communicate and listen. It takes a lot of effort to analyze and synthesize information, interpret its meaning, and share it with others in ways that can be understood. It is common to believe that it is the other person's responsibility to interpret what we mean when communicating with others. It is also common to think that it is more important to contemplate how we would like to respond to others instead of listening to understand and being fully present with the person as we converse with them. It is vital to learn to listen with all our senses and entire body instead of being absent-minded trying to figure out what you want to say. When you make the other person's communication the most essential thing in the interaction process, not only will you be able to be in a state of openness and possibilities, but you will also gain perspective and empathy toward others' worldview.

Behavior Modification

In many instances, knowledge may not be enough. At that point, some individuals need someone to support them in transforming their behaviors about how they react to and perceive conflict, ignoring their blind spot and learning how they took part in creating the situation. Everyone finds it very easy to blame everyone else when a dispute arises and fails to acknowledge what role they took to create the circumstance. Individuals become so convinced that they did not have anything to do to make the conflict. They spend too much energy trying to convince others that they are right and the other party is wrong. It is addicting to want to be right all the time, at any cost. So, they work their way around to gain consensus from others around them to see their perspective and convince others that they are right. Some individuals try to threaten others in the workplace. It is a form of bullying to feel in control of any situation. It is not always easy to modify our behaviors by ourselves because we tend to have tunnel vision of what we want to see in any given situation.

Here is where empathy towards yourself and others can play an important role when modifying your behavior. It is also essential to understand the mechanism of the brain and how it reacts to conflict. Whenever people experience an inter/intra conflict, the mind filters the information through our beliefs, attitudes, and assumptions, which creates the reactions of internal emotions and feelings that impact our physiology to generate behaviors. Our emotions run in our brains at the speed of light. In emotions, we must learn to name them as feelings; stop or perhaps choose the behaviors to transform the outcome from an emotional and

FIGURE 3

CONFLICT INTELLIGENCE METHODS

destructive conflict to an opportunity.

Behavioral modification or transformation requires a shift in reasoning to give rise to possibilities within the situations or circumstances. Having the capacity to expand our view to embrace the other person's interpretation and experience(s) involved in the conflict requires a lot. It requires a moment, a change of perception, learning to shift the ways of being, enrolling others to see your point of view, taking a stand on how you are involved in the conflict. The response you have can also transform a negative conflict into an opportunity for yourself and others. It is about putting all your judgment on a shelf and also dissociating from the idea of finding the wrong or the right in your interpretation of the information. The message conveyed to you acknowledges other people's truth and the meaning of their interpretation of the situation.

It is a journey to apply Conflict-IQ™ to conflict resolutions. It should not be seen as a destination, as every situation or event has its uniqueness. Just teaching scenarios on how to resolve conflict does not take individuals to the point where they feel competent to deal with situations. It is about teaching them to step out of their own way, becoming curious about the other person's point of view, needs, and beliefs, using empathy to create pathways to manage, de-escalate or resolve a situation. Many times, it can only take one person to resolve a conflict.

7

Know Thyself: The Skills and Behavior of a Great Conflict Manager

> *"Mastering others is strength; mastering oneself is true power."*
>
> —*Lao Tsu*

In understanding conflict resolution and how to implement the methods, you need to know who you are. Identity is vital in applying conflict resolution methods. This chapter looks at the traits of a great conflict manager.

Authentic leadership and development come from the ability to understand your principles as an individual. The first fundamental form of power is accepting your abilities as a human being, which further translates to being an excellent leader. As medieval times might term it, knowing thyself is the genesis of thriving in a workplace, whether as a leader or an employee.

Throughout this book, we have seen how different consciousness levels in humans contribute to an organization's success and failure. The highest form of consciousness that is the Unitive Way, allows for the total acceptance of your abilities and the freedom of knowing yourself. This chapter stems from the Unitive Way features that explain the patterns of mastering yourself to get the best out of people.

There is a certain level of respect you command when you are in total control of how you act and react. The soothing feeling that comes from a state of mind characterizes the need to let everyone thrive regardless of inclusion and diversity. The Unitive leader realizes that the organization is not an island; it cannot function devoid of employees. There is a need for a collaborative effort on all sides to ensure an organization's success.

Conflict resolution skills are not exclusively for the managerial levels in an organization, but all employees should learn this soft skill. Conflict is an inevitable phenomenon in any organization, as people from different backgrounds come together to improve the organization's standard. Consequently, there will always be a clash of ideas, cultures, and personal opinions in an organization. However, conflicts should not always be harmful; instead, they should strengthen the bonds in an organization. Relationships function effectively through efficient conflict resolution techniques adopted by members of the organization. As a result of conflict resolution, the parties involved know the do's and don'ts when relating to each other within an organization's context. This allows for the free flow of communication as parties understand each other's limits and barriers in their contributions to the organizations.

Before going into the skills that make a great conflict manager in any organization, it is imperative to understand the routine of conflict resolution. This situation means conflicts are resolved in an organization through systematic steps that mediators follow to maintain the department's serenity and organization. According to Johnson & Johnson (1994), conflict managers, or mediators, as they called them, follow a series of behaviors in achieving conflict resolution, especially in difficult situations.

The first phase of conflict resolution is collecting data. As a conflict manager, gathering the necessary information regarding the conflict is the priority. Objectivity comes to play in this phase as conflict managers need to observe all parties involved without bias. Secondly, probing is the next phase where the conflict managers go in-depth and assume an investigative journalist's role. They ask questions about the crisis at hand to know the best angle to address it. "Saving Face" is a phrase that refers to seeking the solution rather than embarrassing the parties involved, and this phase shows that conflict managers should look for the answers before any other thing comes into play. Discovering common ground entails getting a unified platform for all team members in the organization. Put differently, creating a resolution that suits all members of the organization, regardless of their differences, allows conflict managers to hammer down on the discussions for a solution among all the team members. Based on these discussions, the conflict managers will negotiate with team members on the best option for the organization's success. The conflict managers will then solidify the adjustments by identifying the areas where the team can reach an agreement.

The Skills of a Great Conflict Manager

Conflict managers need a lot of proficiency when trying to resolve conflicts in an organization. These conflicts may be between two employees or between the employees and the organization. Both types of organizational conflict could result from intrapersonal and interpersonal issues that may plague the employees. As seen in previous chapters, conflicts in an organization come from poor working conditions, lack of communication, and stress. Consequently, conflict managers need a high degree of versatility and proficiency since no two conflicts are ever the same. This is because humans are different as they are similar; no one person reasons like the other. Ultimately, the parties involved could be on different levels of consciousness, which means how the conflict managers would relate to them would be different. It is imperative to note that individuals' level of consciousness determines how they will retain and share information. With that in mind, the conflict managers would have to devise new ways of solving conflicts depending on both parties' consciousness levels.

One of the skills that conflict managers should possess is the ability to relieve conflict stress quickly. As a conflict manager, you need to maintain your cool regardless of the situation because who wants to see a leader all decked up in a three-piece suit shouting at an employee. By the time work resumes the next day, you become a trending topic all over social media – lousy publicity. It is effortless to have your emotions all over the place when there is conflict in an organization. Still, as a great conflict manager, you need to first quickly relieve stress. This will help when trying to reason with the parties involved; it also allows you to think of new ways to approach a situation if other areas are not promising. The best way of relieving stress is by doing something that soothes you; some conflict managers listen to music to calm down and keep their emotions in check. There is no way conflict can be resolved with both parties arguing back and forth in the presence of the other employees, but effectively maintaining a calm demeanor will allow you to analyze the issue and proffer relevant solutions that will benefit the whole team.

Another skill that conflict managers need to have in their arsenal is using non-verbal cues effectively. Non-verbal communication is just as important as verbal communication used to resolve the conflict itself. Hand movements, gesticulations, eye contact, and facial expressions are necessary when resolving an organization's disputes. Conflict managers are always free-spirited individuals; they smile a lot; even if you try to get angry, they have a way of making you calm. This is one skill that conflict managers have mastered over the years. Being in charge of your emotions translates to the non-verbal cues you give to the patties. It is possible that your words can be contrary to your non-verbal communication; the conflict might seem resolved but spring up later. You have to be sure of a correlation between non-verbal communication and oral communication when resolving the conflict.

Humor used in the right way can help to diffuse a difficult situation. Conflict managers are skilled in the art of using humor and laughter to resolve conflicts in an organization. In a bid to resolve conflicts, leaders and employees can find a way of infusing humor to reduce the area's tension. However, using humor as one of the skills can be very risky except for versatile conflict managers. The use of humor can backfire if you use it carelessly, making an already bad situation worse.

Empathy might not be a skill to some scholars but taking an emphatic approach is an excellent way to resolve conflicts in an organization. Let us look at this example: Sarah has been working for a beer company for more than seven years and is due for promotion. She performed this last quarter tirelessly and significantly improved the company's revenue through her marketing promotions. However, Sarah did not get the promotion; instead, it was given to another colleague who hardly contributed to the team. Understandably, Sarah is furious. She sees the injustice as a malicious attempt to profile her since she is one of the few women in the company. As a leader and a conflict manager, you have to be able to put yourself in her situation, even if you have never been part of the minority before. Paying attention to the feeling she is expressing and listening attentively to the aggrieved party will, in one way, resolve the conflict. Another way to reassure her is to give a sense of belonging, let her know what she feels is justifiable, and be ready to solve the issue. By listening to her plight, you understand what is causing the conflict, thereby making it easy to address the situation as a whole.

How do Great Conflict Managers Behave?

Managing conflicts can be a grueling rollercoaster for some, as it entails a lot of self-control, empathy, and maturity in every sense of those words. There are days where you want to scream at the parties involved, "Can't you both get along?" but you need to be able to manage conflict without adding more issues to it.

So how do you behave as a conflict manager when conflict arises in an organization?

The answers may be obvious, but the process is not so smooth. It takes consistency to be able to behave as a conflict manager. One way to act as a conflict manager in resolving an organization's issues is by maintaining a healthy relationship. In most cases, what conflict managers do is find a way to foster a stronger bond between or among the parties involved. He or she finds common ground that ties the parties. The conflict manager respects the standpoints of parties involved and seeks to strengthen the relationship first. Many people miss the conflict managerial status because they seek out who caused the conflict and who is winning and losing. As a conflict manager, your priority is to ensure that the relationship is maintained and then diffuse the conflict.

Another way a conflict manager behaves in an organization is by letting go of the past. The best way to move forward is to focus on the present. This state connotes the level of consciousness of all the parties involved, the maturity of the state you are in determines if you can move on from a past hurt. Employees in the unitive level of consciousness believe that the pain is inconsequential as their success is at stake. Leaders should also focus on the present and not the past failures or issues that affected the organization. By focusing on the present, the organization will be able to move forward and achieve its goals and objectives. The unitive level of consciousness that conflict managers adopt enables them to forgive others quickly. Holding on to grudges can affect their peace of mind.

In any relationship, assumptions and generalizations are cogs in the wheels of progress. As a conflict manager, you have to avoid some words. Examples are "never" and "always" when talking about another person in your organization. Generalizations often heighten the tension in an organization, so avoiding these terms will be a smart move. As a conflict manager, you also need to remove personal information from the conflict resolution. This means you should not speak about confidential matters when trying to resolve an issue. It brings distrust and more anger. Conflict managers find ways to handle these issues without getting personal.

Finally, one of the most critical but often neglected traits of conflict managers is the ability to say sorry. This simple word S-O-R-R-Y can make or mar a relationship in an organization. Saying 'sorry' as a conflict manager does not mean you concede defeat. Rather it means you fully understand the other party's plight and further apologize for the inconvenience your actions or inactions may have caused. For example, two employees had always gotten along so well until one of them lost a bet to the other. Mark, who won the bet, never failed to rub it in the face of his friend, Jennifer, and would always refer to her as "sore loser." Jennifer was not mad about losing, but she did not like how her colleague kept rubbing it in her face. However, Mark didn't know, and it became a habit. In an unrelated incident that involved both of them, Jennifer flared up. She started shouting at Mark because he brought up the derogatory name-calling again. So the relationship between both employees was getting strained because Jennifer had begun to dislike working with Mark. To resolve the conflict, Mark approached her to talk about things and listened attentively to what Jennifer had to say, and then he said:

"I am sorry, Jenni. I did not know that was how I made you feel."

By genuinely understanding where the other party is coming from and apologizing for any miscommunication or issue from your end makes you a conflict manager. Conflict managers continuously evolve and improve their ways of handling problems differently, as there are always different situations. Understanding the context, personalities, and level of consciousness will enable you to make informed decisions. Resolving conflicts takes a meticulous but pragmatic approach to achieve its aim. Adopting this chapter's skills will transform individuals into conflict managers regardless of their position in the organization.

KNOW THYSELF: THE SKILLS AND BEHAVIOR OF A GREAT
CONFLICT MANAGER

8

Awareness is the Key to Transformation

> *"We cannot tell what may happen to us in the strange medley of life. But we can decide what happens in us, how we can take it, what we do with it, and that is what counts in the end."*
>
> —*Joseph Fort Newton*

The chapters leading up to this have exposed us to different sides of the discourse. In addition to exploring the other sides, we have seen how these sub-topics contribute to the way leaders and employees resolve conflicts. In retrospect, the aim of conflict resolution in a workplace is to create a comfortable environment that enhances productivity among the employees and the leaders.

Furthermore, to resolve issues and improve the organization's overall productivity, conflict managers employ different strategies for achieving those goals. The preceding chapters examined some of these strategies. For this chapter, we will be looking at the emotional aspect of resolving conflicts in an organization. As mastering conflict intelligence, your ability to maintain composure within, despite what is going on around you, is part of emotional intelligence. This strategy has been employed and even re-modified by scholars over time. Emotional intelligence helps you to build character, stronger relationships, overcome challenges, and thrive at work. Conflict Intelligence can augment your emotional intelligence ability to channel your emotions to the right source to not react to conflict and resolve issues with finesse.

Awareness is one of the skills embedded in emotional intelligence that everyone needs to apply. There are other dimensions to emotional intelligence, such as self-regulation, empathy, motivation, social skills (non-verbal communication and playful communication: humor).

Awareness is the First Step

The state of being aware means you are in tune with whatever emotion is going on inside of you. Conflict managers can pinpoint what they feel and what is triggering those feelings. Awareness also entails considering the way your actions and inactions may affect others around you. In explaining the Unitive Way, the individuals that adopt this lifestyle are aware of their emotions and the factors that trigger certain behaviors. They also understand how important it is to consider other people's feelings and opinions when speaking. Awareness is the point of self-realization where individuals can fully identify themselves as part of a community of leaders; thus, there will be some form of skill in their nature.

There is no way you can fully resolve conflict without understanding who you are as a person. Awareness is the point where people know their limits, biases, priorities, and outright negativities. You cannot fully understand someone unless you know yourself to a certain degree. Inevitably, you cannot see the caliber of issues you might face at work on a particular day. Still, you can determine how you react in any given situation. Some people find humor even in the most upsetting situations; for them, it diffuses the situation from escalating any further. While for others, taking a walk might help them come to terms with what is going on inside them. Awareness as an aspect of emotional intelligence is the best method or approach through which individuals can come to terms with feelings like anger, sadness, fear, excitement, etc. In essence, the state of being aware comes first before any other form of emotional intelligence. Without understanding yourself, nothing can flourish.

Self-regulation and Awareness

Self-regulation is the uncanny ability for conflict managers to keep their emotions in check no matter the situation they find themselves in. This ability takes excellent discipline because not many individuals can pull it off, keeping their emotions in check when a volatile problem arises—regulating emotions, feelings, and attitudes for the organization's growth. Awareness in the scope of emotional intelligence is when emotional feelings and reactions are kept in check in the workplace. Here is an example: an argument ensues in the office due to a brainstorming session's clash of ideas. Suddenly, there is a lot of uproar in the department; words thrown from different angles; the department is messy. However, you maintain your cool by becoming aware of the place you are in and the conditions. Suppose you are due for a raise, and there is uproar. In that case, awareness provides context and the requirements to regulate your behaviors. So even if the other person is wrong, you will most likely end up apologizing just for peace to reign.

What happened here? The ability for you to be aware of the situation provides a possible condition for self-regulation. The kind of consciousness you possess shows how well you handle your emotions. It tells of who you are and what you stand for, making it easy to regulate emotions. Another example will be a pastor who is in a corporate establishment; no matter the conflict that ensues, you might never see him bat an eyelid. It is because of his awareness of his identity, which provides the context for him to react.

Empathy and Awareness

Empathy is a skill that conflict managers use in understanding the viewpoint of the other party. It is the ability to put yourself in another person's situation to properly understand a behavior's premise. For conflict managers, the ability to see things from other people's perspectives, which is a feature of the Unitive Way, is a form of empathy. In attaining the unitive standard of living, accepting different ways of solving issues is one of the tenets of this consciousness level. As such, conflict managers can see things from an angle they never thought could be possible. By accepting new methods of trying something, you invariably put yourself in another person's shoes. Empathy can be born out of the personal experience that the conflict managers might have experienced in understanding the other person or channeling emotions in seeing the new angle.

Awareness allows conflict managers to become more empathetic about a situation. By weighing and evaluating all the conditions, conflict managers resolve conflicts by seeing things from another perspective. For example, suppose an employee is denied a raise because of the underlying factor that he or she is black. In that case, there might be severe conflict in that department. It takes an empathetic individual to understand the issues that humans are going through to resolve the conflict. For minorities, it is hard to envision yourself in their shoes; the only time one can relate to that situation is if you have ever felt alone in the world before. Awareness empowers leaders to assess the problem by sending someone from the same minority group to address the situation or recognizing the issues at hand and making adjustments. Some of the adjustments that leaders can make in the inclusion and diversity review on company policy can show empathy to the minority in an organization. Awareness allows conflict managers to think about how others will feel after their actions.

Social Skills and Awareness

Social skills entail the ability of conflict managers to resolve issues without degrading other people. Effective communication is the process that allows for conflict resolution; this means conflict managers have to be able to disseminate information clearly and concisely. Effective communication involves recognizing specific social structures and cues that aid the free flow of the process. It means for communication to be effective, and there are other factors aside from the oral form. This situation is where social cues, which are non-verbal communication and humor, come to play. Social skills take a deep understanding and awareness of the environment, the people, the words uttered, and the feedback. Social skills also involve the ability to know when to talk, interject, and make general comments.

In an organization where there is a lot of diversity, being aware of the social structure regulates your behavior towards an employee. There are certainly some things you cannot say if you are talking to a person of diversity, especially when trying to resolve a conflict. There is a particular cycle of events that shows the relationship between awareness and social skills. Let's take a look at the diagram below to understand the process fully:

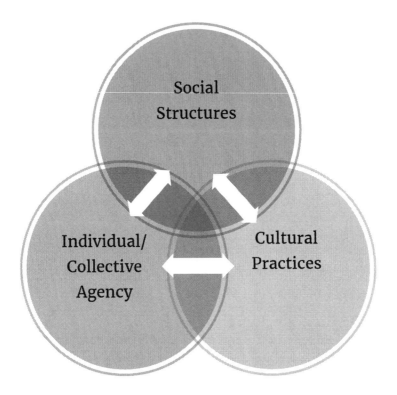

In resolving a conflict in an organization, the conflict manager utilizes emotional intelligence by becoming aware of the social structure that exists between the parties. In this first phase, the conflict manager is mindful of the person's cultural background or people trying to resolve conflict. In understanding their cultural background, the mediator gets to know their level of consciousness also. It allows the conflict manager to understand how best to converse with the parties. Secondly, the awareness phase allows the conflict manager to regulate his behavior since some things may be offensive to the other party. This is necessary, especially when talking to the minority in an organization.

Understanding how best to resolve conflicts in a social setting is a skill that mediators have developed over time. Being aware also means taking note of the non-verbal cues the other party is passing across. Breaking eye contact, nibbling on the shirt, and nodding the head are all different forms of non-verbal communication. Understanding what they mean in their proper context will help resolve conflicts quickly. Social skills are ways of resolving disputes in a particular context; therefore, no two methods are the same. It might be a similar incident or conflict that occurred. Still, the social context is different based on the people involved. Therefore, you need to consider the socio-cultural context before mediating an issue so there won't be any offense.

Humor is another aspect of social skills through which conflict managers help to reduce tension in the organization. Humor entails a great degree of skill and proficiency when being applied to sensitive situations such as conflicts. Knowing when to use humor is an impressive feature of a mediator's game plan. Humor can heighten the tension and can also solve the issues quickly. Self-awareness is the first step in utilizing humor as a weapon for diffusing conflict. The process of being aware and knowing when to use humor is a careful study of the parties involved. The awareness stage also makes it possible for the mediator to know what type of humor will suit such a situation. Since humor goes in different ways, understanding what can diffuse the conditions, whether gesticulations, words or even physical contact. Each form has a significant role to play in a different context than you may use it.

Self-awareness in the workplace actively influences self-regulation, empathy, and social skills (Church, 1997; Shipper & Dillard, 2000). There is an element of self-awareness to the different forms of emotional intelligence that conflict managers use in resolving conflicts. You will inevitably need to communicate with yourself before making some decisions in any relationship. A workplace is also a place where individuals have to be in tune with their inner self before making decisions and carrying out tasks. It is on this level of consciousness that employees and leaders carry out their daily tasks. As such, being aware of conflict situations allows individuals to make informed decisions that center on their progress.

In retrospect, awareness is the key to transformation in a person, other people, and an organization. Self-awareness, being aware of the people around you, and considering the social context is the catalyst for transformation in any organization. If everyone thought about how their actions or inactions would affect others and consistently worked on it, there would be reduced organizational conflicts. In an inevitable dispute, the resolution becomes quicker as the conflict managers have experience at the organization's different levels. The transformation of each department in the workplace becomes seamless. Self-awareness in all administrative areas makes the transition into the Unitive level of consciousness an easy path for employees and leaders. Awareness is a critical element in conflict intelligence; in general, it connotes putting others in the scheme of things as you work in an organization. Since there are people with different backgrounds and principles to life, accommodating their feelings, beliefs, ethnicity, and experience is awareness.

Consequently, the manner through which you speak and act towards them will be different. With this in mind, awareness becomes a condition that puts individuals in check. The state of being conscious keeps us from going above and beyond our relationship with people at work. A relationship takes understanding and emanates from being aware of the situation that brings people together in an environment and the people themselves. Understanding these key elements will help leaders and employees make better decisions for the growth of the organization.

Educational Process

> *"Every leader must have a plan to handle conflict in his or her organization. Leaders need to resolve conflict at the source, strengthening relationships through a better understanding of the expectations on both sides of any conflict."*
>
> — Orrin Woodward.

The preceding chapters show that conflict resolution goes beyond terminology and an actual system of procedures. Conflict resolution is more mental than it is physical. Many solutions are made in the mind before we ever get to speak to the other party.

In this chapter, you will learn the educational process of resolving conflict. Conflict resolution entails a conglomeration of steps that instruct people on making informed decisions when there is a conflict. Also, you will understand the principles that ensure the conflict resolution process is complete.

There are various steps leaders have to go through in their minds before they make any decisions. For leaders, the right mindset comes as one of the most pivotal stages in conflict resolution. In adopting the right mindset, leaders should always be proactive when a conflict arises. It is crucial to continually be prepared to deal with people from different backgrounds and intellectual dispositions. Bearing this in mind, anticipating conflict is an excellent start in having the right mindset to tackle it.

Proactiveness and preparation when conflict arises lead to being able to deal with the issues directly. Conflict leaders face problems head-on and attack them directly. Talking to a person is the best way of resolving any conflict. As much as technology has simplified the standard of living, it is expedient to work on people's issues rather than texts or phone conversations.

Furthermore, as a leader, you cannot allow the conflict to grow into something much bigger. No one wants a feud that takes the whole company down. Ironically, some disputes have been resolved without them getting out of a particular department. It takes the right mindset to focus on the greater good of the organization than proving a point to the other party – most times, and it is not worth it. In maintaining the right mindset, leaders do not spread the issues, gossip, or problems that may cause other people conflicts. Organizations that have employees criticizing others behind people's backs will have a hard time dealing with resolving conflicts. No matter, leaders always find a way to protect the other party's reputation, no matter how heated the conflict is.

FIGURE 4

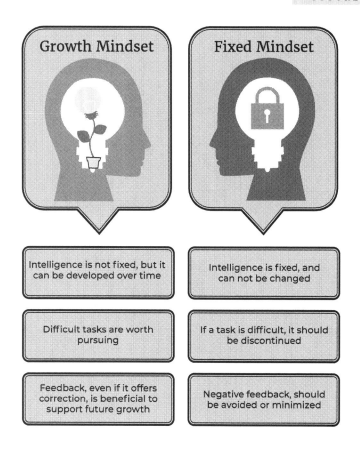

Principles of Conflict Resolution

The educational process involved in dealing with conflicts in an organization talks about the various conflict resolution principles. Different scholars have come up with their lineup of how conflict resolution can be resolved. However, in this chapter, we will look at the step-by-step processes involved in conflict resolution and the roles leaders play in each stage. The figure below puts this process in perspective:

FIGURE 4.1

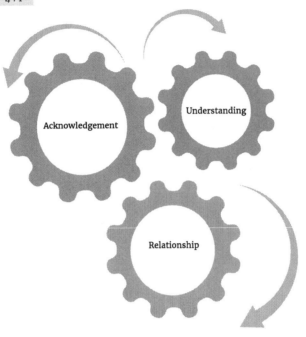

Relationship

In understanding conflict resolution's learning process, as a leader, you need to realize that the relationship between the two parties is worth more than the conflict itself. As humans, we thrive only by relationships with other people, whether at work, at home, in church, in a gathering, or anywhere we find ourselves. We cannot do anything on our own. In the same vein, valuing relationships in the middle of a conflict is one way of resolving the issues. In understanding that the relationship matters more, the communication will be different. You can make statements like, "I am here because I want to make things right between us." These statements come out of love and respect from both parties, recognizing that their relationship is one way the organization can thrive. Through effective relationships, there is a free flow of communication, which further leads to productivity.

FIGURE 4.2

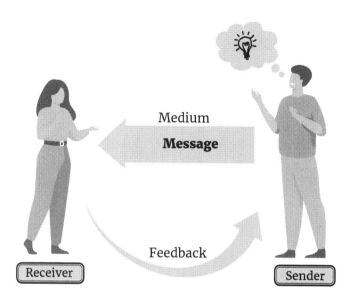

Medium

Message

Feedback

Receiver   Sender

Understanding

Now that there is an established understanding between you and the other party, you need to seek knowledge of the whole situation. Here, you need to first focus on understanding the other party, and often what you feel caused the conflict might not be the issue. Asking the person directly and inquiring what led to the conflict in the first place can help resolve the dispute faster and prevent a future clash. However, for proper conflict resolution to occur, you need to listen attentively. Listening is a great communication tool that leaders must possess. You have to mirror the words of the other person, which shows that there is effective communication. The feedback you give will show if you were truly listening. It goes beyond the cliché remarks of "yes" or "I understand."

People want to know that they are heard and understood. Only then can they be ready to listen to the other party and consequently resolve the conflict. There has to be a corresponding answer from the other party that denotes that you have truly understood what was said.

Acknowledgment

This does not only relate to when you are wrong, but you have to acknowledge that there is indeed a conflict immediately from recognizing the conflict. It might sound absurd, but many people prefer working in denial that there are no real issues, only for those issues to hit the person where it hurts—in essence, accepting that there is a conflict makes the leader seek solutions to solve them.

Furthermore, you have to be able to stop and apologize. It is a memorable leadership trait, whether it was your fault or you were just slow in resolving the issues. Leaders need to take ethical responsibility for their actions and inactions; it helps build trust among employees. You will be surprised by the level of trust between you and the employee after acknowledging the conflict. To make the workplace a healthy environment for everyone, acknowledging, apologizing, and moving on from the issue are necessary. As a leader, forgetting the conflicts and transitioning to other essential matters helps the resolution of conflict. No one wants a leader that continually reminds you of the issues you once had; it tends to get overbearing.

Control

Not all conflicts will be calm; some issues might be so emotionally draining that regrettable words might begin to come out. As much as this is the human way, leaders have to exercise control over their emotions in every conflict situation. Have you ever heard people play the "I am also a human being" card? Of course, we're all human beings, words get to us, but leaders need to have tougher skin.

In growing a tougher skin, you should be able to communicate your feelings without letting your emotions get the best of you and avoiding assumptions and generalizations of staying in control of your feelings. Another practical way of controlling your emotions is by taking a break. This does not mean you are not attending to the conflict at hand, and it could be some minutes to gather your thoughts and cool off before responding to the other party. Leaders have mastered the art of taking a break from the conflict to think about constructive ways of making their opinions known.

Surprisingly, in taking a break, you can come up with a joke that reduces the tension. Regardless of the technique, you use to get the other party to listen to you, controlling your emotions ensures the conflicts are resolved faster.

Resolution

Suppose you are a neutral party trying to act as a mediator; maintaining neutrality from the beginning till the end aids resolution. Identify the places that both parties need to work on because it takes one to start a conflict but two to mend the fences. You point out these areas have to be Specific, Measurable, Agreed, Realistic, and Time-bound for a proper resolution to take place.

In finding a resolution after a conflict, you need to be patient. These two people are very different from you in so many ways; understanding each of them might take a great deal of patience. Without this, you risk the chance of rushing into resolving an issue that requires a well-thought-out approach.

Another element to a resolution that many leaders note is how you handle conflicts in your daily life. The success of helping others through their conflicts depends on how well you can manage conflicts in your life. You can apply this level of awareness to the situations you find yourself in at the office. As explained earlier, become conscious of the conflict, acknowledge that it is there, and make provisions in resolving it.

There is a caveat in resolving conflicts in an organization, especially if you are the mediator. After successfully helping to solve the issues, encourage both parties to also resolve conflicts on their own. Through the use of some of the techniques employed in their situation, they can become mediators. It builds their leadership skills. One thing that makes an organization successful is if all employees take responsibility and see themselves as leaders.

In seeking a resolution, you have to ensure that both parties agree. It might seem that from the relationship stage till this point, everything has been settled. But if there is no agreement between both parties, a proper resolution will be missing. It means leaders go the extra mile in ensuring a bond emanates from the conflict that would have caused issues in the department. When scholars say not all conflicts are harmful, it means how leaders resolve the conflicts such that it affirms their relationship and agreement.

Affirming the relationship and seeking an agreement between the two parties in an organization are two ends of the same stick or two sides to the same coin. There has to be a balance; leaders affirm that the two parties' relationship is more significant than any conflict. Consequently, it is engraved in the employees' minds that their relationship at work needs to come first. Thereby, any conflict that arises again can be solved because they need each other to excel in the workplace. Therefore, an agreement is required at the end of the resolution process. Agreeing that both parties will not make the same mistakes in the future strengthens the relationship.

In a way, conflicts resolved in the right way affirm relationships on every side. This is what you, as a leader, need to focus on. As much as you need to acknowledge the conflict, you should not dwell on it, instead focus on how it can be solved and how both parties can move on amicably. In any organization, the relationship among coworkers determines success. It is through a stable relationship with people that you can achieve the goals and objectives.

In conclusion, this scenario will help you put into perspective the need to focus on affirming the relationship before resolving the conflict.

No matter how close mothers and their kids are, there is always bound to be conflict that will brew between them. In movies, we watch mothers quarrel with their teenage daughters about the boy they are going out with or get their grades up. Imagine a situation where the mother prevents the girl from seeing the boy. We have seen that the teenage girl might jump out of the window in several movies to see the boy eventually. After she gets caught, there is a heated argument, and the conflict bursts out. To resolve the conflict, the mother and the daughter will realize that their relationship is far greater than their conflict. When the door opens, and the mother creeps into the daughter's room to apologize, both of them apologize.

The mother might ask, "Do you love him?" to get a grip of the whole situation, and there the girl talks while the mother listens. This exchange goes on vice versa till both parties agree on a few things. It may be for the daughter not to spend too long outside or for the mum to meet the boy she has been seeing.

In the same vein, the organizational conflict has to be resolved in the same way. Leaders need to show people that both parties are essential to each other and find ways to agree—the relationship in the workplace overtakes anger, guilt, and conflict.

Understanding the Path to Resolution

Leaders will know that resolving conflicts in an organization is not a one-way street. It never is. Most times, you have to take some detours, speed bumps along the road, a couple of stops, and checks before getting to your destination. This issue happens because no two conflicts are the same, and the people are different most times.

To act as a mediator in your workplace, understanding the path to resolution is the key to resolving the conflicts themselves. As much as affirming the relationship and agreement are entry and exit points, respectively, there are other areas you need to address. No matter how different the parties and the situation are, it takes the same path but different strategies. For you to become an effective mediator, dynamism has to be your watchword. Leaders are dynamic in their approach to resolving conflicts in an organization.

Finally, effective communication is necessary for an effective transition to each course on the path to conflict resolution. So, if it means listening to give the appropriate feedback, then it has to be done. Without communication, there might be gridlock on the way to your destination – conflict resolution.

10

Re-tooling the Brain

> "Talk back to your internal critic. Train yourself to recognize and write down critical thoughts as they go through your mind. Learn why these thoughts are untrue and practice talking and writing back to them."
>
> —Robert J. McKain

This chapter dives into the mind of the leaders and employees in properly understanding how conflict resolution works. It is necessary to see how the mind works when trying to implement conflict intelligence methods.

Have you ever seen someone get so angry that they start to shake? The more they vent, the more vibrations they make. Situations that trigger anger in an organization are always bound to happen to us one time or another. Evidently, in our lives outside of work, someone or something will get us angry. It could be your wife after you made some arrangements, but she didn't fulfill her end of the bargain, and it could be the Wi-Fi refusing to connect for about 20 minutes with a deadline looming.

Similarly, some colleagues can get on your very last nerve in the workplace, and the only option you have is to snap right back at the person. You are eventually breeding conflict in the department. The battle of succumbing to your anger and calming down is usually fought and won in the brain. So, what happens in the brain?

FIGURE 5

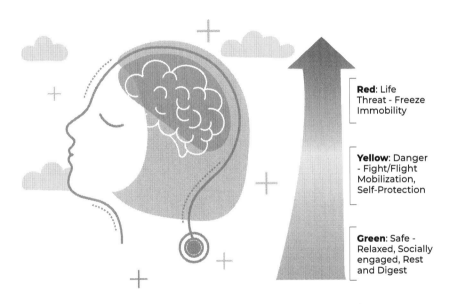

Red: Life Threat - Freeze Immobility

Yellow: Danger - Fight/Flight Mobilization, Self-Protection

Green: Safe - Relaxed, Socially engaged, Rest and Digest

When conflict arises in an organization, emotions immediately start to rise, the reaction in the brain settles in the amygdala, which is situated near the hippocampus of the frontal lobe. Consequently, our brain will immediately release and increase our cortisol level, which causes most people to react in seconds. As this happens, the anger builds up while blood rushes to the brain. This reaction occurs so fast that the brain becomes stressed. The hippocampus is affected severely, resulting in a term known as brain fog. This term means a state where individuals cannot think appropriately, usually when there is conflict. As all these occur, the body begins to react, causing sweat, uneasiness, vibrations, and other peculiar traits. The blood flow increases, muscles become tense, adrenaline surges through, and your instincts kick in to react. In a matter of minutes, the whole department might be trying to separate you from almost hitting the other person.

There are a lot of activities in the brain. Activities happen before you respond to the trigger that your colleague has set off. Regardless of the anger trigger, what separates leaders from ordinary people is their ability to control the anger. You can take a break and re-tool the brain before making any decision.

Re-tooling the brain explains the way leaders become mindful of the situation at hand. The level of awareness that they feel in the moment helps them make informed decisions. Religions like Buddhism refer to this state as mindfulness. It is an effective way of resolving the conflict in the brain before it starts.

The Process of Re-tooling The Brain

For conflict resolution to occur in an organization, you have to control your thoughts. Without it, the reactions you will give could be catastrophic and may repeatedly happen before you can reason clearly. Re-tooling the brain is very important not just in the organizational structure but in life generally. The ability to free yourself from being taken over by your emotions is a great way to start the journey of being a leader. Re-tooling the brain is not a simple task because we have to drop some life-long habits that require discipline and patience. Many leaders have passed through and are still passing through this process of re-tooling the brain.

Level of Consciousness

This is familiar territory for us as we have seen how different levels of consciousness have come into play in life and an organization. Re-tooling the brain starts from being conscious of your environment without bringing your assumptions, prejudices, likes or dislikes, and other opinions. But you are instead open to new possibilities from the environment that you are in currently. This does not mean your colleagues or the organization are trying to change your principles or viewpoint on life. It merely means you see things for the way they are, accepting that there are other possibilities asides from what you already know. As some may relate to the concept, mindfulness, or awareness, deals with being in touch with the various aspects of where you are as an individual. In an organization, being aware of the setting, participants, dialogue, and other elements helps you understand the situation better and avoid conflicts.

Do you get angry when you are trying to talk to a teenager about some problematic life concepts? Of course not! You only make them understand what you are saying in terms they can relate to. This means you are aware of the situation and avoided any form of conflict by communicating in a way the other person will understand. In the same vein, being aware of your colleague's disposition will prohibit you from making some particular statements that may be termed derogatory. Mindfulness breeds understanding.

The Power of Meditation

People often think that meditation is an elaborate exercise that takes a long process before anything is possible. However, the simplicity of meditation makes people believe there is more to the practice. It is merely the act of stopping to evaluate things. You do this in a calm and serene place in your mind, away from the conflict and the triggers. Meditation does not just happen when you close your eyes; it takes a conscious effort and energy to weigh all the options in your head before making a decision. When conflicts arise in an organization, the leader can take a few minutes to breathe. He or she is not trying to figure out what to say or how to act. The leader is just taking himself out of the situation by looking at things from the outside. He or she asks himself what is happening, what they see as wrong, and the cause. By asking those questions, the situation is much clearer, and the resolution can be made quicker.

Most times, meditation is flawed by trying to get a solution after some moments of deep thinking. It is more of a state of being and a sense of being aware of the present moment. You need to sit down and see yourself for where you are. There is no rush to get to the solution but look at things by what they currently are. It is not about harmonizing the past and the future but focusing on the present moment. This helps you remove any other things that cloud your judgment, which will hamper your decision-making.

Grab Every Detail

To be in a state of mindfulness, you need to grab every detail. It is crucial to becoming fully aware of your surroundings, the people, the conversations, and other elements. As humans, it is effortless for us to drift into a blank space of oblivion—a state where we do not think of anything but wander like a lost sheep in a forest. However, snapping out of that nothingness and taking a moment to breathe helps us to return to where we were. We can re-tool the brain and become mindful by grabbing every detail as we go along.

In an organization, paying attention to every detail as we work helps us be more aware of ourselves and others. It is as simple as breathing, notice the simple things first, and then transition to the seemingly complex things. Regularly doing this will help you stay in a state of consciousness that allows you to appreciate everything and function more effectively in the organization. Breathing cannot be overemphasized at this juncture. By breathing, you take control of anxiety and anger that might be starting to build up. Taking long deep breaths helps you to salvage the situation. Leaders need to breathe when conflict arises. It allows you to see the case clearly and to assuage the anger.

Breathing also plays a massive role in concentration at work. There are distractions everywhere you look. However, practicing breathing can help you navigate through all the issues that come with unawareness and conflicts. The more you practice, the more you explore areas that you never knew were present. The breath is the connecting force between the mind and the body. The back-and-forth communication takes place through the breath. Therefore, paying attention throughout your day allows you to stay ahead of any conflict that may arise. It will also help in finding ways to resolve inevitable disputes in the workplace.

Change your Worldview

- How do you see the world?
- What do you think of your colleagues?
- What do you feel they think about you?

Your perception of the world influences how you will act, interact, and speak to other people. The way you view the world tells a lot about your personality. In re-tooling the brain, changing how you view the world will be a big step to achieve a stable level of consciousness. Suppose you believe that other colleagues are out there to get you or are at the cafeteria planning your downfall? In that case, it indeed will affect your productivity and relationship with them. To correct whatever notion you have of your colleagues, you can take the bold step of spending time with them—asking them if they have plans, not in an intrusive way but friendly. Participate at get-togethers. The reason you feel weird about people is because of the lack of time spent with them. After spending time with colleagues who were once evil, you realize that some shared interests and values strengthen the relationship. This newfound friendship then translates to the work environment; thereby, generating more fluidity, and conflicts can be resolved quicker.

You should always give room to get to know others, understand where they come from, what motivates them. As explained earlier, getting to see things the way others see them is not about truncating what you stand for. It is more about accommodating other people's feelings, mindset, values, religion, worldview, and other principles before deciding. There is no fear of being sucked in on your path because you believe in learning from people. If people consider others' feelings in an organization, there would be more resolutions than conflicts. Instead, people are trying to show that their way is better, and you must not see it that way.

Recognizing that we can learn when considering other people's lives can make an organization and the world a free space—a place void of discrimination, bias, and segregation. As such, accepting a Unitive Way of living allows people to see the world the right way.

Be Patient

If we all can have this virtue, there would be a lot more peace in the world. In re-tooling the brain, patience is highly required. Not just for yourself, but when dealing with others. The ability to accommodate other people's beliefs and values takes a great deal of patience from your path. Leaders are extremely patient in their dealings with people; they consider each employee's opinions and calmly see each issue.

Patience is the key to being aware of the situation; it allows one to take a deep breath, meditate, and look for the best solutions to the conflict at hand. In an organization, you especially need patience since you are dealing with different people. The way you work is certainly not the same way they do their work. Patience is also evident in every conflict resolution stage; you need to be patient to understand the other party. Consequently, patience is the bridge leaders cross to meet the other party. It helps them understand and proffer the best solutions to the problems in an organization.

Lay Aside Every Weight

Have you ever felt tension from your colleague that is a bit unexplainable? Agreed! There was a bit of conflict, but it was resolved. However, there is still something a bit off with her/him. It is like there is still some hidden anger somewhere, but each time you approach them, they say, "It's nothing." Most times, the other party has not forgotten about the conflict; maybe some words that were spoken cut deep, and that person has not been able to move past it.

As a leader, you have to be able to let things go. Holding on to a particular word or conflict can act as a weight dragging you back each time. It might sound like a cliché, but without letting go of the pain and the hurt, you cannot truly move forward. There would be a lack of productivity and blurred vision. All because of some conflict that happened weeks or months back.

Furthermore, it takes a tremendous amount of energy to hold a hurt. Your body and brain are stressed; anger builds as you constantly remind yourself of the damage. However, letting go of the pain and the conflict will relieve your entire system, and you step out of the warped mindset that caged you for long.

Without letting go, you keep going in a strange circle over and over again. This process hinders you from achieving your goals as an individual and the company's objectives. Letting go is a vital part of re-tooling the brain; humans hold onto things with their minds. It is not surprising that if a girl gets dumped at a parking lot, each time there is a parking lot in view, she remembers her breakup. However, letting go is not an instant procedure; it takes time and considerable effort. One way of letting go is to be aware of where you presently are. Your consciousness and happiness at the level you are makes you forget what happened before. The most important thing that matters is what is happening at that very moment.

Therefore, leaders focus on the situation at hand, disregarding how they felt before or how they think later. But they think about what they are feeling at present and dwell on that.

11

The Wabi-Sabi in Conflict Resolution

*"There's a crack in everything;
that's how the light gets in."*

—*Leonard Cohen*

Many people see conflict as a dangerous thing in organizations. This chapter seeks to change that mindset by showcasing how beautiful conflict can be if the correct methods are implemented. This chapter is a culmination of the conflict intelligence methods that have been expounded.

Many people stumble on the concept of *Wabi-Sabi*, whether in movies, social media, magazines, or just in interactions with other people, but do not understand the true essence.

Wabi-sabi is an ancient Japanese term explaining how to find beauty in the imperfections of life. Some writers tag the name as "*Flawed Beauty.*" It is a lifestyle that appreciates anything and everything for what they represent, whether in the woman you love or the car you drive. No matter what surrounds your life, the ancient Japanese concepts relate to enjoying every moment regardless of its shortcomings.

It is almost like being aware of what is present at a particular moment in time, accepting the way the world is regardless of the COVID-19 and the other issues plaguing the world right now. There are still beauties in the imperfection that is life as we know it presently.

The wabi-sabi concept is embedded in the idea of conflict resolution. It just takes a little bit of uncovering to see. Although, much of what we have been discussing thus far relates to seeing conflict beyond what it is. It is a door to a plethora of opportunities in the organization and for leaders. So, how is it possible that conflict in itself is a flawed beauty, or how can we view conflict resolution as a beauty amid a storm?

The Right Mindset

Many people indeed see conflict as a bad thing in an organization. They see it as a cog in the wheel of progress from time to time. Some people describe a conflict as holding a storm back with a broom or going into the ring with a 7-foot giant - all indications of the impossible odds conflicts weigh on us. However, this book seeks to remove the veil before your eyes by showing how conflict is not all bad but doorways to remarkable changes in the individuals' lives and the organization. What if a conflict is a remedy?

You ever feel that talking sometimes does not resolve the conflict, it might feel that way. Although there are strategies that help you transition from one stage of conflict resolution to another, the other party might not be ready. So, what do you do then? There is no way you can force the person to talk, and it only makes it worse. The beauty in conflict is the ability to take a step back to see what the issue is and tackle the problem.

At times, talking may not be the first point of contact when dealing with someone in your office. You might have tried talking at different points of the day, but nothing changes. However, when you get a small gift with a little note, the person becomes warm enough to talk to you and resolve it. The wabi-sabi in conflict is the ability to get to know someone beyond the ordinary work relationship lines. Conflict strengthens the bonds of friendship if people view it the right way. It would help if you had the right mindset to be able to see the beauty in conflict.

The Beauty in Conflict Resolution

Conflict resolution is the pathway through which humans establish stronger bonds in the workplace, at home, or anywhere we find ourselves.

Let's look at this scenario to deduce the beautiful side of conflict resolution. Kim had always been bullied during significant parts of her life. Throughout her time in high school, she was either body shamed or beaten. The torrid time continued as she went to college, although by her final year, Kim was able to gain some ground. The turmoil for years had made her feel the world was against her; Kim was heavily guarded and didn't have friends. All she believed was to get into her office and do her job. She avoided confrontations like her life depended on it. Unfortunately, a conflict ensued between her and another colleague. As a result of her conservative state, Kim reacted defensively, and she brought guns to a knife fight. It was not until the colleague's resolution stage learned of her past and how it had always affected her. It was more apparent now; she was not reacting because of what he said, but as a culmination of her past years.

There is Always More

Conflict resolution is more about the relationship than it is about the conflict itself. We think we are seeing the real deal on the surface, but there is an iceberg underneath that can sink any ship. The wabi-sabi of conflict resolution allows mediators to break down walls put up by people due to past experiences. We are all products of our experiences, but sometimes people enable these experiences to define who they are and what they represent. This is why employees in an organization do not make as many friends or purposefully segregate themselves from the pack. Therefore, the conflict might not be the problem but how the person feels in their former organization. It could be the things that come out in the heat of the moment reminded the other party of her abusive father. It could be anything in the real sense, but there is always more to the conflict than we see on the surface. The beauty therein lies in people's ability to let their guard down. The weight that they have held for many years can be stripped away through conflict resolution. Conflict resolution is a subtle yet powerful tool that changes the lens through which many people view the world. There are endless reasons why conflicts ensue in organizations. Still, the ability to uncover the truth behind the mystery makes you a leader. Recognizing what the conflict is about makes a huge difference in resolving the issues.

Self-Realization

The beauty of conflict resolution also comes with self-realization. Conflict resolution helps individuals self-determine where they are in a particular moment and how their present experiences can help them become better. Before the conflict resolution stage, many people think they are blameless in the heat of the moment. It usually is the case, as they feel the other party is wrong and did nothing to make the situation worse. Typically, you hear little kids say, "But he started it." These kids grow up with that mindset and blame the next person for conflicts in an organization. The hidden beauty in conflict resolution is it helps people recognize when they are stuck. Let's look at this example below.

A father tells his seven-year-old daughter to stop bossing her other sisters around after weeks of talking to her and trying different strategies; there is no change. Bear in mind; the father has tried to speak to her calmly, yell, and buy gifts.

After weeks of futility, the sisters still feel bullied daily. The father goes in to switch off the child's light then proceeds to speak with her. "I do not know how to get through to you, Laila, and I have never raised a 7-year-old before. I am sorry I yelled, I hate it, actually, but I want you to know you mean the world to me." The father says this without trying to seek a response and rests his head on her shoulders. Laila then sobs slightly and says, "Dad, do you think I am pretty?" It was not until they discussed and resolved the conflict that the father knew she suffered teasing in school. So, Laila took out her frustration on her siblings and her dad.

Recognizing that you are stuck is not a weakness. It is you trying to solicit help from the other party to resolve the conflict. The father would have thought he was blameless and that it was all his daughter's fault but realizing that he could not move forward without resolving the conflict not only brought them closer than before but helped her deal with her issues. Mindfulness is the product of conflict resolution, and that in itself is a beauty. At that moment where you are stuck, there is a realization of your poor state. Probably, you said some inappropriate things under the guise of resolving conflict. This happens when people in the organization think they have fixed the conflict, but the other party has not moved on. Self-realization helps you make further adjustments to your character. Looking inwardly to find a way to accommodate the other party is one of the beauties of conflict resolution.

Taking Responsibility

Conflict resolution allows people to take responsibility for their actions and words. Taking responsibility for your actions is such a beautiful thing, as it makes you vulnerable. Vulnerability is not in any way a sign of weakness but an indication that you are aware of what is going on. It shows that you want to change and accommodate other people into your space. Responsibility also removes the entitlement mentality, the feeling that everyone owes you. In taking responsibility, communication is imperative. The way you communicate will show your intent, whether in your non-verbal cues and gestures – every detail counts. Some scholars refer to taking responsibility as ownership. It translates to owning what you have said or done in a bid to resolve a conflict. Ownership is not easy; you realize that you were the trigger that set off the other party. Most times, the feeling of regret creeps in; however, for your relationship with your colleague to flourish, you need to take responsibility.

Accepting the Realities of Life

Furthermore, conflict resolution allows us to accept the harsh realities of life, the truths we are too afraid to tell ourselves. This

THE WABI-SABI IN CONFLICT RESOLUTION

beauty can be obscure, as it changes the mindset we might have built for years. Life comes with some bitter truths, like not all relationships are happily ever after, or not everyone will like you. Understanding these truths will help you resolve conflicts better and become more in tune with yourself. It is okay for a few people in your organization not to like you; it does not mean you are a terrible person or terrible at your job. It is the way life is. Conflict resolution helps you uncover this truth. One familiar truth life teaches us is we are all not perfect. As humans, we are bound to make mistakes; sometimes, we might raise our voices when we are not supposed to, say things we do not mean, or act a certain way. Therefore, conflict resolution helps us become better human beings by seeking ways to become more aware and accommodate other people who are not perfect. By accepting this truth, you become more patient with people and foster more significant relationships with them. In essence, accepting the realities of life also means the loss of an idea.

Building Trust

One significant theme in conflict resolution among people is it builds trust. By letting our guard down in seeking a solution to a problem, we allow others to see the real person at the other end of the conflict. There are no more flaws left to hide, no stories to tell, and nothing left to hide. Conflict resolution takes a lot of trust to happen. It enables you to share something like how bullies made you feel with your colleague. The sharing of past experiences to move on from the present conflict takes confidence and trust. The beautiful thing about this is that it makes us stronger while helping us break free from the chains of guilt, fear, sadness, and pain. The foundation of conflict resolution lies in trust; without it, there cannot be any communication form. Let your feelings be known and respond because you can relate to the issues that are raised. The goal of communication is not to force your ideas down people's throats but to have a shared identity and a common ground where the conflicts are adequately resolved.

The Importance of Wabi-Sabi in Conflict Resolution

As we have seen that there are elements of the Japanese concept in conflict resolution everywhere we go. More importantly, the significance of wabi-sabi is to appreciate what life offers us greater joy; this is what conflict resolution seeks to do.

In any organization, conflict resolution helps people value work relationships. People have a renewed sense of participation, and there is a newfound joy for work. After the conflict between Kim and her colleague has been resolved, Kim will look at the world differently this time, not from the stress of bullying, but the appreciation that there are still good people in the world.

Conflict resolution allows us to be more self-conscious and aware of other people who contribute to our lives. Leaders are exemplary characters; they can see beyond the issues that plague a department or the organization. To them, there is always something beyond the surface, and uncovering it is the only right way to move forward. Leaders see the beauty in everyone, and they believe they can learn from wherever they go, whether at work, at home, or online. There is no limit to their acquisition of knowledge.

In retrospect, there is a lot of beauty in conflict resolution; it takes an in-depth look to see how beautiful the process can be. To see the beauty within, you have to open your eyes and appreciate people more. Treat people how you want to be treated and understand that there is only a limit to what you can achieve without a good relationship.

12

Re-tooling the Brain
Behavioral Transformation

> *"To change a habit, make a conscious decision,*
> *then act out the new behavior."*
>
> —*Maxwell Maltz*

This chapter will discuss the extent to which conflict resolution helps in transforming individuals' behavior. It will also shed light on the essence of the self-determination theory and how each component influences behavior. Furthermore, the need to be self-conscious and aware of other people and surroundings contributes to transformation in behavior. All these aspects will be examined as well.

Effective conflict resolution techniques empower many leaders to become confident whenever conflict arises. There is a calm breeze that blows through their offices when a chance to become a mediator comes. It is not like they are looking for conflicts in their organization. Still, the opportunity to improve lives through conflict is what they relish. Conflicts in organizations are regarded as an opportunity to improve lives and the state of the business. Now, imagine if every employee adopts this leadership mentality of conflict being a doorway to greater possibilities. As a result of the right mindset in which leaders engage themselves, their behaviors are refined to resolve any kind of conflict. Leaders are in total control of their emotions, as they use logic to calmly dissect the issues and see things from others' perspectives. This is where self-determination theory comes in.

Self-Determination Theory in Behavioral Transformation

The feeling of total control and competence in one's abilities can be attributed to the self-determination theory. The self-determination theory posits that two significant factors elicit changes in behavior. According to the scholars, for an employee to be happy and transform in their actions, these two factors have to be in place: the extrinsic and intrinsic factors.

Firstly, the extrinsic factor is the reward or recognition attached to the work that is being done. Compensations, benefits, or incentives are how employees transform their behaviors in the workplace; it is only normal to be motivated by promotional opportunities and pay raises in an organization.

Secondly, the intrinsic factor refers to the innate feelings that occur within the employees that motivate them to change. The intrinsic factor states that for an employee to be happy at an organization, there are three elements they must possess. These elements are as follows:

- Autonomy
- Competence
- Relationship

The elements mentioned above play a vital role in the behavioral transformation of any employee in an organization.

Autonomy refers to the need for independent working. It is the feeling that you have control over yourself and your surroundings—the need for the employees to be in charge of their decisions. Autonomy, in a general sense, can be termed as an independent existence. For employees, organizations give them autonomy by telling them to choose which area they want to work from or which branch they want to be situated in. However, autonomy does not come easily; employees have to work to get that opportunity. It takes some degree of hard work, diligence, and patience to become autonomous in an organization. So, how does this affect behavioral transformation?

After years of slaving away at your desk, writing many articles, you finally get a senior editor position. The position comes with more money, an award, and, more importantly, autonomy. There is a new level of confidence that rolls through your sleeves. You walk into your office in the morning. You earned this moment; therefore, wear it like a champ. Many people feel powerful, strong, more competent, and confident when they become autonomous. There is an absolute thrill about being in control of your time, emotions, surroundings, and even the people around you. After all, you are their boss now. The feeling of accomplishment transforms your behavior in and around the office.

Let's look at another scenario if you used to eat at the cafeteria as a former student. Now that you are a teacher in the school, there is no way you will eat where the kids are eating, will you? Another scenario that is even more relatable is when you become an adult and move out of your parent's house. You have your apartment; there will be a transformation in your behavior. You cannot do the same things you used to do while at your parent's place. In retrospect, behavioral change becomes evident when there is autonomy.

Competence is the second intrinsic factor that transforms employee behavior. It refers to the feeling of success or the possibility of success in an activity. Competence is the ability to be confident in getting the job done, maybe even do it better than other people. This factor emanates out of experience on the job and a lot of hard work. Your experience in handling conflict makes you very comfortable when an issue arises. You never see a leader panicking when there is a conflict, whether group conflict, dysfunctional conflict, or any variant of conflict.

Although no two-conflict situations are the same, neither are the parties involved. But the sheer confidence of handling a conflict before gives you an impetus to solve the issue yet again. Imagine on your way to the hospital; you drive the car but fear the worst as your wife's water just broke. Your friend is in the car, but he is as calm as the sea. Everyone is screaming, panicking since there is a little bit of traffic. Suddenly, your wife yells, "I am going to have a baby," You respond by screaming. Your friend in the car sees that she is about to go into labor and spring into action. The only thing he says is, "keep the car steady," as he pulls your wife's seat back, he tells her, "Don't worry, I am a doctor." All nerves after that sentence disappear immediately as a few minutes later, the baby is born.

One thing competence does is change the behavior of others towards you. Suppose a conflict resolution coach like a therapist was to resolve some issues in your marriage. The response you will give the person will be different from what you will tell your friends.

Relatedness or relationship is a sense of belonging or connection to a particular person or group in an organization. We cannot survive without being part of a team at work or in life. Creating relatedness is as simple as asking colleagues out for a drink after work. It could be participating in the traditional game night at a colleagues' house. Either way, belonging to a particular group has a way of affecting your behavior at work. There is no way you can stay motivated on your own; the right kind of people around you help to improve your life.

These motivational processes that have been explained give rise to the changes in employee behavior. Both extrinsic and intrinsic behavior facilitates a difference in people's disposition in life and an organization.

How the Roots of Conflicts Affect Behavior

As much as conflict resolution influences positive behavioral changes in an organization's employees, some factors contribute negatively to the way people behave in an organization. It may be in the way employees relate with each other or despair resulting from an internal conflict.

According to Crawford, Usadel, Shrumpf (1991), there are three conflict roots: Limited Resources, Unmet Needs, and Different Values. These factors can affect how employees behave daily at work, in the house, and even alone.

Limited resources entail the time, money, and property of an individual. Each resource affects behavior significantly when something interferes with it. If you are running late for an interview, the tension that builds in your body can be unbearable. You become susceptible to internal and external conflict. Let's add some more spice to this scenario.

What if, as you get into the elevator, there is a jam. You and the other three occupants are stuck on a particular floor with the PA system stating everything will start in five minutes. While waiting, you realize the interview was meant to have started 30 minutes ago. In that anger, you tap your feet with boiling rage. Then one of the occupants sees this gridlock as fate brings both of you together. He moves in to try to get your number, but at that point, you are not ready for any romantic entanglements. So, what do you do? You tell the poor man off.

That is not who you are on a regular day, but time was not on your side; the interview had started, and someone was trying to get your number. Time is a factor that can alter people's behavior in a matter of seconds; this could lead to conflicts as well.

Have you ever been a bit low on cash? The feeling is terrible, to say the least; you might not be the most fun person at the office that day. All because your rent is due and there is no money coming in until payday. It can be a bit frustrating trying to work and relate with people based on these scenarios.

Unmet needs are more or less the consequences of limited resources. Everyone has unmet needs ranging from physical to spiritual. There are unmet needs like rent overdue, unpaid hospital bills, failing to graduate, or failing the work's promotional exam. These needs alter the mood and the behavior of the individual, making them unproductive. These needs drive our actions, and the absence of these things in our lives can be frustrating. In the workplace, the unpaid salary can be the reason for the conflict. Consequently, employees are no longer happy with the conditions of the workplace. The productivity levels will begin to diminish with more conflicts starting in groups and departments in the organization.

Finally, different values are one of the primary reasons there is a behavioral transformation in the workplace. Most organizations are equal-opportunity employers, which means they hire people regardless of their sex, age, color, race, religious background, and other characteristics. As such, each employee has a different cultural experience, which makes their worldview different from yours. However, understanding each person's boundaries and values would alter how you behave. Ironically, you could be permitted to make some comments and act some specific way when you are with a particular group and not do the same thing in another group. What is permissible in one department might be frowned upon in another.

Addressing these values in other people becomes a recipe for behavioral change in an organization. This ability only comes alive when you are aware of other people around you. It does not mean being a psychic and trying to read minds. But in relating with others, you should accommodate their expressions and feelings in the workplace. Recognizing the emotions that come up when interacting with other people will also alter your behavior as well.

Emotions, Logic, and Empathy

These three elements further contribute to behavioral transformation in an organization. Emotions emanate from values, principles, and codes of ethics that individuals stand for at a particular time or place.

Logic is the ability to reason clearly and deduce the roots of the problem or conflict. Most times, leaders use logic to control their emotions; they figure things out devoid of any additional element clouding their judgment.

Empathy is how you put yourself in other people's situations, especially when they are aggrieved. Experienced leaders find the right balance between these three before they act and make lasting decisions. They all have a role in changing leaders' behavior, but in resolving conflict, the proper harmonization of these elements is imperative. Empathy is a trait that allows you to accommodate other people's feelings when resolving an issue. As much as everyone wants to feel justified by their actions, the ability to take a pause and reflect on what the other person has to say takes strength. Real strength lies in being empathetic to others regardless of the situation.

However, as a leader, you have to be careful when trying to resolve conflicts. This point is another instance where your behavior changes. It is easy for mediators to be neutral in another person's conflict. But sitting on the fence in their conflict is sometimes impossible.

With the practice of self-determination theory, leaders can be in the best control of their emotions while transforming their attitudes. Conflict resolution aims to bring out the best in people if the proper techniques are followed. People's lives and relationships change dramatically and for the best when both parties do the right thing.

Significantly, conflict resolution empowers employees to become better people in the organization and life. The resolve of severe issues in the organization brings colleagues together and helps them see the best in each other. If their salaries are paid after the conflict, there will be a difference in character by the next day.

13

People Analytics

> *"Instead of suppressing conflicts, specific channels could be created to make this conflict explicit, and specific methods could be set up by which the conflict is resolved."*
>
> —*Albert Low*

This chapter will give you insight into how People Analytics plays a vital role in an organization's growth. Also, organizations benefit from data-driven methods and how People Analytics comes into play in conflict resolution.

Organizations are in business to create services and goods to make a profit, and people drive business. Human relationships in the workplace are a significant part of what makes a business work. The fact is that when placing humans together, dynamics happen that could take the energy and the focus of each individual away from benefiting the bottom line of any organization. The emphasis for many decades has been placed on reaching human engagement in the workplace. Although we can find significant research, we are still far behind from knowing what drives employee engagement. In my opinion, we have missed the mark in looking closely at the nature of humanity in the workplace. We also need to unveil and realize that organizations try to hide or sugar-coat prevalent human conflict in the workplace.

Human conflict happens in any situation where facts, desires, or fears push or pull participants against each other or in divergent directions. Conflict can be unpredictable and is inherently part of what happens when you have multiple people interacting at any given time, especially in the workplace.

Workplace conflict can happen unbeknownst to the boss and upper management. It can run its course until it indirectly affects a system in the business. The organization tends to think that the human resource department and its legal counsel are the safety net to control its human conflict. They do this by creating policies and procedures that only focus on disciplinary processes and the organization's protection—therefore neglecting the human side of the conflict and leaving it as an open wound latent to damage employees' engagement in numerous ways. Thus, these systems to discipline employees might be creating leaky holes that are hijacking organizations' bottom lines. For an organization to adopt other mechanisms to address human conflict in the workplace, it is imparted before spending attention and resources in these efforts. They must seek to find the type of human conflict in the organization and understand the efficacy of the existing systems used to address these issues and the lateral effect of unsatisfied employees. The standard disciplinary procedures used in the workplace do not address how to get people back together to work; instead, they only punish employees.

People Analytics is used to shed light on these areas of

concern. Organizational leaders can have an honest look at areas hindering the overall organizations' profit. Collecting different types of data lets HR and leaders form a holistic view of the organization.

Analyzing the human conflict in the workplace and developing a conflict management system design might be the missing key to driving loyalty, trust, and engagement among employees in the organization.

The Role of Technology

Over time, technology has gradually taken over the title of man's best friend. There is virtually nothing we do without the perks of technology. From eating to banking transactions to everyday survival, without technology, the world as we know it will be obsolete. People are not shy to say they depend solely on their phones, tablets, or laptops. Human beings have transitioned into a state where conversations are more digital than physical, with new technological advancements emerging. Man's insatiable nature has made us want even more from technology; we demand more from the source daily.

Organizations all over the world are also enjoying the benefits of depending on technology. Can you imagine how it was back in the day? To forward a document to another location could take hours, but now with a click of a button, the other person gets the information. Technology has collapsed the excuse that distance had always been a barrier. Now, the barrier is the person using the technology. But in essence, technology has improved the way people conduct their business in many organizations. The information technology, marketing, sales, branding, and even customer service aspects have been heightened with technology's power. Now, information is processed 100 times faster than it used to be as everything now runs on data. HR personnel does not need to go through vast loads of paperwork to look for an employee's file. Today they search records on their system and find them.

Data is the currency through which organizations and life itself runs. The amount of information on digital space is mind-boggling. There is such a massive amount of data stored in organizations' clouds and storage systems, which can be retrieved and used at any point in time. Data and man go hand in hand; wherever people are, so will data be.

Organizations have large amounts of people's data stored up in their records for emergencies or general information. People Analytics are indispensable when we are talking about organization intelligence. People Analytics is the pathway through which organizations and the employees can cohabit and perform their duties with very minimal conflicts.

Why People Analytics is Essential to an Organization

Organizations understand that their strength lies in People Analytics; without these two components, improvements cannot occur. One of the reasons People Analytics is essential is that organizations use them to make better and informed decisions. Using People Analytics, organizations use a data-driven approach to manage people at work. This method was shot into the limelight some ten years ago when organizations used different metrics to understand the kind of people they had in their organization.

The organization is continually capturing data on employees through the increase of analytical capabilities. Nowadays, computers can analyze millions of data each day, making it easy for organizations to effectively manage their employees.

Another reason for the importance of People Analytics is the Return on Investment (ROI) it gives the organization. There has been an increased ROI since 2014 with the use of the analytical system to make informed decisions in investments. Organizations have found that it is like having two peas in a pod. It has also led to an increased profit in every organization where the method has been effectively utilized. The effective management of employees and using each person in the most suitable role in the organization only yields greater productivity. People Analytics shows leaders the best people to handle a position; with this in mind, if the right people are in their most preferred job position, work becomes more productive. Imagine someone gifted in writing but being on the graphics design team, there may be little or no productivity if the person is not design-oriented, and that is a totally different case from when that employee writes for the organization's website; there will be an increase in productivity, as well as higher profit. If everyone in an organization functions in their best positions with the right kind of motivation, success is inevitable.

People Analytics as an organization's driving force makes it easy to spot the right employees for the job. These components show how effective employees are relevant to their job descriptions. With People Analytics, promotional opportunities are made more available to deserving employees. As a leader, you can identify hidden talents internally and externally suitable for some specific roles. These roles might not be related to their job description. Still, they help contribute to the organization in one way or another. People Analytics also helps leaders in an organization select applicants that are best suited for hiring. Here is a scenario: the organization is seeking a new copywriting executive, and about 50 candidates are applying for the job.

This process could be grueling, sitting through 50 interviews;

however, People Analytics helps you streamline the candidates to the best few ones. The questions and tasks you will give to the aspiring employees will be based on understanding them better and improving your organization. Leaders also use their external network to recommend more people that will be suitable for the role. Organizations give detailed descriptions of the prospective employees' responsibilities to their network to see if the right candidate can come from them.

In the same vein, People Analytics are viable options to look at the people who do not contribute as much to the company's growth. Imagine getting the groceries after one hectic day after work. As you get some of the supplies, you realize that the milk is expired. Right there, the office managers check the aisle where you got the milk and throw away all expired milk. They replace them with new ones in a matter of minutes. People Analytics makes it easy for organizations to spot rotten eggs or expired milk in this case. Ultimately, you are in business to make money; therefore, anyone holding you back has to be cut off. This is why People Analytics plays a vital role in identifying people who do not contribute to their success.

Also, People Analytics helps leaders identify the best teams to pair each employee. It gives the organization a clear vision of which employees will be the best fit to be put into a team. Working in groups is essential as it helps understand each member of the organization and increases productivity. It makes the work more fluid, and there is a vast expanse of ideas floating around the organization. As crucial as fixing employees into teams, choosing the right team to function is no longer an arduous task. With data-driven methodologies, leaders based on past and present trends can choose like-minded organization members to form a team. Organizations sometimes give employees the autonomy to choose their groups based on their experience. However, the formation of groups is as essential as the members of each group. It is like the leaders are managers of a soccer team, and each game night, they have to pick eleven players that can play together and bring home the trophy. Similarly, organizations do this to see the employees that work better in teams and maximize their potential.

Employees can get personalized training, developments, opportunities based on job descriptions and requirements. Leaders can deduce what is best for the employee's career based on the data generated.

How People Analytics Benefit Employees

For employees in an organization, they receive certain benefits from the harmonization of data and people. Through analytics, employees have a clear career path without any distraction or interference. With relevant data, employees can see the places they can work and thrive in an organization. Even if they were right in one particular field, data helps place the employee in the most suitable environment where success is guaranteed. The data collection offers employees career opportunities that are streamlined to their personality, a function that is second nature to them. Through relevant training and tasks, the employees have a clear vision of what they want to achieve.

Analytics is also the tool through which the employees become versatile and prolific at their jobs. People Analytics empowers employees to find the best fit for their expertise and thrive in it. Employees can answer any question related to their field and proffer solutions to that field of endeavor. Another plus for employees is the ability to detect when the next big move is going to be. Data allows employees to make informed decisions on their career transitions.

People Analytics has made organizations' and employees' lives much better by making informed decisions based on relevant updates through information gathering. Now organizations are updated on recent happenings and changes in the lives of their employees.

So how do all these come into play in the conflict resolution discourse?

How People Analytics Influence Conflict Resolution

Let's clarify that not all conflict is destructive; some conflict can be a source of energy that fosters creative and resourceful problem-solving. Unmanaged conflict, however, can have detrimental effects on the overall net earnings of an organization. Let us look at the following startling statistic in which People Analytics can bring a solution.

A 2008 study done by the CPP Global Human Capital Report found that U.S. employees spent 2.8 hours per week dealing with conflict. This amounts to approximately $359 billion in paid hours (based on average hourly earnings of $17.95), or the equivalent of 385 million working days. Another statistic indicates that when an office worker deals with the stress associated with the interpersonal conflict with coworkers or supervisor, the output of worked hours diminishes to less than 3 hours per day, totally using an average of 15 hours per week (The American Institute of Stress 2019).

The adoption of People Analytics data to collect information across the organization's board helps understand the workforce. People analytics can enable leaders to identify actionable insights to improve workforce retention and recruitment. It is essential to highlight that it is necessary to concentrate the information and collect data that only impact the area we would like to find solutions to drive the business forward. A clear objective that the data is sought for the organization's betterment will build the necessary trust among those in the organization that might be affected by collecting the data and the solutions that might come out of the final analysis.

People Analytics' advantage is that it can demonstrate if the human resource department's typical systems to address employees' conflict are working or not. It can also show opportunities to implement a conflict management system that could save the company money and increase employees' satisfaction, loyalty, engagement, and productivity.

Without people, data is entirely useless. Analytics become one ample space of information with no one using it. Similarly, we are nothing without data, bank transactions, emails, and social media. Everything that technology has given us becomes empty. This is why these two components, although they can be mutually exclusive, are stronger together.

Data allows leaders to stay abreast of situations involving the employees. It gives organizations the right tools to be able to handle and manage the employees. With this, leaders can make informed decisions that will influence the behavior of the employees positively. Leaders use data to help improve the lives of employees and enhance the credibility of the organization.

Wisely choosing what data to collect is fundamental to solution-driven people analytics. Observing trends on the data can depict information that can be used to establish metrics that predict if the Human Resource process based in the organization is either decreasing or increasing the adverse effects of human conflict in the workplace. A quantifiable solution in which the data can also be measured is essential in this data analysis.

If you can improve employee experience in the workplace,

you'll improve your performance as a business. It is critical to take a balanced, long-term approach to implement People Analytics in an organization to assess the efficacy from a holistic econometrics' perspective and not from a short-term process. The core idea of People Analytics is to keep employees invested in the business both implicitly and explicitly. People analytics provides organizations with the ramp to upgrade the employee experience and increase employers' performance to maximize profit. Every employee's interaction with the organization is a data point and could glean exciting insights. The idea is to transform the relationship that HR has with employees – to help HR become and be perceived as more than just a support function but rather a place where employees are treated as humans.

14

Conflict-IQ™ System Design

> *"The degree to which misconduct remains unidentified is determined by how well employees are screened, trained, and supervised. Recognition, corrective action, and training are necessary steps to cultivating and preserving a healthy and profitable company."*
>
> —*George J. Ramos*

The need for employees to be skilled in conflict resolution is all this book has been discussing. This chapter seeks to elucidate how the Conflict-IQ™ system design is imperative in any establishment's organizational culture. Conflict intelligence and its tactics have ways of empowering the employees. Therefore, all employees can change the way an organization behaves inwardly and to its clients as well.

This chapter should open you to understanding your current skill level in conflict resolution. The measurement of your ability to resolve workplace issues places you in firm control of developing new strategies to maintain peace and tranquility. In essence, without determining where you are in the scheme of things, there is no way you will know what areas to improve on when conflict arises. We will be looking at the various areas in which employees are trained to enhance conflict resolution and make it a part of the organization.

Why is Conflict-IQ™ System Important?

Let us take a trip down memory lane, shall we? In the first chapter, we talked about the Unitive Way and how leaders have attained this consciousness level through consistency. The Unitive Way embodies a sound and clear mind that accommodates other people's beliefs without contradicting your principles. We exposed the concept as the heightened form of self-awareness in which many great leaders operate.

Now we will make a play from that chapter to understand why training employees in conflict intelligence is vital for the organization's growth. A human being is a conglomeration of all their interactions, communication, and shared beliefs with other people. This means that we are shaped and influenced by the people we see, meet, and interact with. Conflict-IQ™ is essential for employees because it teaches them how to interact and communicate with other staff members. An organization comprises many people from different backgrounds, nationalities, languages, and other differentiating factors. Organizations expect employees to get along with one another regardless of their cultural discrepancies.

Conflict-IQ™ teaches people to consider others when communicating. In essence, for employees to thrive and maintain tranquility in the organization, there has to be an understanding and mutual respect of other people. Conflict intelligence informs the employee how to behave, considering the gestures and verbal comments they can make in front of their colleagues. Empathy is not just shown when the conflict's resolution begins but in your communication and dealings with another employee and client. In an organization, there is always a diverse community where people from different backgrounds come together. This means for employees to survive and thrive as a unit, there needs to be shared understanding despite their cultural differences. The Unitive Way employees embrace each other's differences and filter out the ideologies you do not condone. For example, the fact that someone is of a different religion does not mean they are wrong. The essence of Conflict-IQ™ is to imprint in employees' minds that it is possible to co-exist with or without the world's boundaries. Of course! There would be conflicts, but understanding each other's differences makes it easy to resolve quickly.

Imagine this scenario; A woman walks into a clinic with her two sons, who are probably hungry because they are screaming at each other. She is a Hispanic woman struggling with her hair while also trying to calm her two boys. The noise is discomforting not just to her but to the employees in the clinic. One of those plagued by the noise is the Front Desk Assistant, who is already having a bad day as she has to deal with a possible backlash from her boss for forgetting to submit her report. As the kids are now rolling on the floor and throwing tantrums, the front desk lady comes through; she talks to the Hispanic woman in a rather hostile and unfriendly tone to get a hold of her kids because it is "a working environment." As a result of the tone in which the front desk assistant talks to the mother of the two boys, she just stares at the front desk lady, uttering nothing. Suddenly, the front desk assistant raised her voice while assuming that the boys' mother's silence was because she probably did not understand English. Rather than deescalate the situation, the front desk assistant went on to say, "These people just act poorly, especially with their children."

Interestingly, the Hispanic woman understood English correctly and heard the front desk assistant the first time but chose not to respond, perhaps as a way to manage the conflict and prevent it from escalating into something worse. However, the derogatory statement the employee made did not go down well with the Hispanic woman. The next day the assistant was suspended without pay. That situation could have been handled better by the front desk assistant, and she may have become friends with the Hispanic woman and her two boys.

Conflict-IQ™ system design helps to caution employees regardless of the situation that transpires. No matter how obnoxious the children or the woman were, the employee should not have made such a statement. So, she put herself in danger, and the reputation of the clinic was also at risk. The essence of training employees with the Conflict-IQ™ system is to equip them to understand how best to handle a situation without prejudice based on race, color, sex, social class, culture, and language.

Conflict-IQ™ goes beyond the basic conflict resolution techniques and creates an atmosphere for critical thinking in the employees' minds to understand their organization's response to conflict. Through practical training on Conflict-IQ™ , employees can deduce how organizations deal with conflict, thereby making it easier to resolve issues that involve the management. Furthermore, the methodology also offers a platform to discuss different approaches to conflict resolution in an organization.

Through thinking about solutions rather than apportioning blame, employees find it easy to devise new solutions to solving problems.

If every employee has an upgraded Conflict-IQ™ , it will create an environment that promotes open dialogue during conflict resolution. In this space, people will be free to air their opinions without fear, malice, or prejudice. The goal will be to resolve any conflict in the organization. Therefore, employees are equipped with the correct technique to control their anger and respond to others when they are angry. Anger is part of the human makeup, and one way or another, you will get angry in the workplace. So, what do you do? Would you bring the house down because you haven't submitted a report? Conflict-IQ™ helps to keep you in check.

Organizations invest money in conflict resolution training with questions, demonstrations, and teachings on the discourse to provide a healthy workplace for employees. An organization depends on the peace and progress of the employees and without them getting along. As a result, organizations fall short of their bottom-line. These training sessions are essential for the reasons mentioned above and more. Identifying the best practices for communication and active listening is one of the training that organizations give employees.

Identifying the Causes of Conflict

An indelible area that Conflict-IQ™ in an organization exposes is the root causes of the conflict. Conflict resolution training affords employees the ability to identify the most common causes of conflict in an organization. Training employees with Conflict-IQ™ shows each role a party plays in aggravating and resolving the conflict. It could be that some employees enjoy shifting the blame onto others in the department or the organization as a whole. These employees have issues with taking responsibility for their actions. Consequently, the employee will be prone to making excuses and not deliver the job on time.

Another issue which training employees in conflict resolution help to uncover is not dealing with minor irritants as they surface. One of the mistakes employees make is not correcting problems when it is in its early stages. The issues might be minute, like playing music in the morning just when work is about to start. Some employees enjoy listening to music while working. It helps them to focus on their work while others find it a distraction. Conflict-IQ™ will allow both sets of employees to reach a compromise if within the same proximity. But if this is not addressed, there will come a day where one of the employees will snap, causing a real conflict in the department. Training employees allows them to deal with an issue that could pose a threat in the future as quickly as possible.

Am I the problem?

The Conflict-IQ™ methodology aims to help employees identify techniques to employ in resolving a conflict without damaging the relationship between parties. The organization can influence the employee's decision-making by training them on conflict resolution intricacies. The onus rests on the employee to get better and gain Conflict-IQ™ to improve themselves and perform better. It is only normal for conflict to arise in an organization. Look at the multicultural landscape that is paraded in many organizations. There would be misunderstandings over certain principles, work ethics, and other nuances in the organization. Tempers will flare, conversations will be heated, and issues will arise. So, what do you do?

Are you the kind of person that makes threats and ultimatums during a conflict or an argument? Let us look at the scenario of the Hispanic woman with the two boys. The matter could have been handled a lot better but imagine the employee threatening to throw the woman out if she did not control her kids. Now that can spark the triggered woman into a frenzy and probably cause shouting and screaming, consequently disrupting the clinic's order. Some employees need to refrain from threats and ultimatums in their organization. The Conflict-IQ™ system is designed so that employees look inwardly and find the issues that spark conflict.

Another issue employees face when dealing with conflict is not sharing the person's problem to clear things. Conflict-IQ™ systems in organizations provide insight into the ways employees should act and react to guarantee a resolution. Employees in an organization should endeavor to talk things out with the other party when they are calm and collected. Conflict resolution must be between the two parties through talking and finding a middle ground. In sharing the problem with the other person, you need to be aware of your role in the conflict, what you said or did not say that added to the issue, amongst other things. The truth is, most times, we are not absolved of the blame in a conflict. It comes from self-realization and awareness to recognize what must be done to salvage the relationship between the employees and the clients.

Using the scenario in this chapter, the next time, the Hispanic woman comes into the clinic. The first thing the employee needs to do is apologize for the derogatory statement she made to the mother. However, the other person could have done better with her kids, notwithstanding the employee shares in the blame. Most of the time, our need to reprove other employees can come in a misinterpreted way. Many factors can cause that to happen, but Conflict-IQ™ gives people an understanding of how to make their feelings known without instigating a conflict.

In retrospect, organizations need to regularly screen and train employees on conflict resolution as much as it is essential to hire the right people for the job. Based on their expertise and experience, the company's long-term growth must have sufficient Conflict-IQ™ and make quick decisions when conflict arises. What is the essence of having a great employee who does not get along with other colleagues in your organization? With constant complaints of their attitude and actions in the organization, it lessens productivity. This is one reason organizations need to start investing in programs that improve their employees' conflict resolution skills. Set up scenarios where you put employees in a situation to see how they will react to a conflict. It allows you to know where the organization is and how they best understand the organizational culture. Some organizations go with the motto "the customer is always right." Training employees on the best ways to handle conflict can save your reputation a whole lot of damage.

The conflict resolution system is a continuous process that employees need to embrace for them and the organization to move forward. Top organizations providing quality products and services have built their reputation by handling conflict the right way. This won't be possible if the employees do not imbibe the organizational culture and exhibit phenomenal conflict resolution practices. The need to train employees in this organizational culture aspect is as vital as their organization's work.

15

Engagement, Performance, Inclusion, and Culture

> *"The better able team members are to engage, speak, listen, hear, interpret, and respond, the more likely their teams are to leverage conflict rather than be leveled by it."*
>
> —*Runde and Flanagan.*

In the previous chapter, we looked at the necessity of having conflict resolution training in the organization and how employees can benefit. We understood how conflict resolution plays a dominant role in promoting the employees' organizational culture and spreading it to the clients. It is necessary to have the background information on the perks of conflict resolution training to flow with this chapter.

Employees are integral parts of any organization's growth. Without them, the objectives of the leaders will be null and void. No matter the organization's inspiration and vision, if the right sets of employees are not available, there would be chaos. The big question is, how do you get the right employees? We have already seen that conflict resolution training is one approach to absorb the organizational culture and equip employees with the proper techniques to tackle conflict and resolve organizational issues. However, this chapter will shed light on how organizations can motivate employees to become leaders in their own right to resolve conflicts.

The elements discussed in this chapter are essential in motivating employees to become better and evolve as staff members and humans. For an organization to grow and improve, the employees need to improve as well. The principles of engagement, performance, inclusion, and culture are interconnected as they point in the same direction. Each element's position creates a comfortable environment for each employee to work freely and thrive independently and collectively. If one employee in a department is not growing, the productivity of the whole team is compromised. Therefore, to understand this chapter, each element will be exclusively explained.

Engagement

An organization thrives on the uniqueness of each employee under its workforce, whether they are of Asian descent or African descent. The peculiarities of each employee are harnessed to produce the best results for the organization. This is why organizations specially train employees on different techniques of handling conflicts. However, as always, the dilemma is, what is the best way to engage the employees? How do you get them interested in learning how to be better at conflict resolution?

Most times, those benefits do not last for long. An engagement coach is saddled with the responsibility of developing informal or formal conflict resolution programs for employees in an organization. Their job is to provide a viable platform that caters to intervention services to individuals, employees, managers, and other staff members. These services are centered on interpersonal conflicts, work stress, change of management, clarity of roles, interpersonal competencies, among other issues that hamper healthy work-life balance. The engagement coaching process entails a detailed conflict management system that offers guidance to all organization levels on the best ways to handle issues. The engagement coach is not restricted to a particular level but to all the departments that make up the organization. The appointment of a skilled and versatile engagement coach is necessary. They help create an environment where each employee and manager can meet and discuss upcoming issues that pose problems. This method shows transparency in the organization's management style, engaging the employees and prompts for the right environment.

The engagement coach must also work on sensitive issues that employees cannot speak about concerning age, gender, racism, and other relevant matters to the laws and applicable agreement. The aim is to talk about those issues to recommend strategic solutions. Employees enjoy the fact that the organization is right behind them on matters. The organization has to show support to each employee, reinstating that everyone is equal in the workplace. It allows employees to participate in the daily activities of the organization. Organizations also need to conduct follow-up reviews to see the progress of employees after resolutions. Also, to ensure the resolutions are firmly implanted and the threat of retaliation is removed, organizations need to conduct these reviews.

The need for engagement in an organization is essential not just for conflict resolution but also for understanding the people or the employees who make up the organization. The engagement coach includes people from different cultural backgrounds and minorities to escape any form of prejudice, discrimination, and segregation in the organization. Employees function better when there is an organizational culture that accommodates people from different phases of life. By engaging the employees, people get to know their likes and dislikes, making it easy to understand what you can do and say around them. Sometimes it is possible to misconstrue the identity of an employee until they talk. The engagement process inspires transparency, accountability, and productivity.

Performance

Most organizations' multicultural and dynamic nature needs to be made to engage every staff member to ensure an environment suitable to work and enjoy working. Properly engaging employees can only lead to better performance. When the issues and opinions of a diverse culture of people in the organizations are heard, considered, discussed, and resolved, there will be greater participation. The employees will begin to feel that the management listens to them; hence, each team member's performance will be improved. The other parts of this chapter also point to the overall performance of the employees and the organization. The Inclusion and culture of the employees in the organization enhance the performance of the people. This will be elaborated further. But first, let's look at this scenario and see how engaging the employees can yield improved performance.

There is diversity in culture in most organizations. There

are White, Black, Hispanic, Asian, and Arab people all working together. However, this is not the deciding factor; the main issue is the disparity between the male salaries and the female salaries. The latter believe they work as much as the former and deserve to be paid more. This starts when one of the female colleagues overhears another male employee talk about his salary while trying to get lunch. The shock on her face was even more glaring when she told her other female counterparts. With the new info, the women refused to work, showing they contribute a considerable amount of work to the organization. Hence, the management reviews the issue and sees the immediate salary increase of all the organization's female engineers. The action by the management will spur the women to put in more effort now that they can see the management listens to their demands.

Conflict resolution is a formidable way of improving the performance of employees in an organization. When there is peace in an organization, it makes for a clean environment to work effectively. For employees to thrive, there has to be a comfortable environment that accommodates all employees to speak and work freely without fear of intimidation.

Inclusion

We are all different. It is from these societies that we have teams of people who work in an organization. These sets of people have backgrounds that may or may not be similar to what others have. Although there might be some shared experiences, there would be some disparity. Inclusion is employees' participation in the activities, benefits, and operations of an organization without prejudice.

Every employee wants to be part of the team; they want to feel that sense of belonging, and so does every human. Inclusion usually goes hand in hand with diversity in an organization. Employees' Conflict-IQ™ is enhanced when the principle of inclusion is embedded in the organization's policy. This stems from an organization stating it is an equal opportunity employer, which means they offer the same opportunities and benefits to all employees regardless of their differences.

For an organization to grow, all employees need to be included in the daily activities and meetings. The importance of including employees in the decision-making process of the organization cannot be stressed enough. Conflict is reduced when employees are included regardless of their skin, age, gender, social class, cultural background, and other factors. When employees see that organizations are about creating an environment that promotes their growth, productivity in performance is heightened.

To level the playing field, organizations view the differences between employees as uniqueness and resources in enhancing their overall performance. However, sometimes employees cannot shake off the prejudice in their voice or gestures towards another employee. For example, if a man has some kind of prejudice about women in power, he might not take it well if he is meant to report to a woman daily. This, in turn, will cause a bit of conflict in the days to come. The sheer disdain that he has to get permission to do things from his superior, a woman, is degrading to him. However, the way to go about this is by listening actively and being aware of your actions.

Most times, throwing prejudice aside allows us to see who they indeed are, not for their accent, color, age, sex, or social status. Inclusion goes beyond calling everyone for a meeting but being empathetic to how people considered minorities are feeling. If there's a meeting and all men have spoken, it would be wise to let a woman also speak to get another opinion. It is the little things that show Inclusion is adopted in an organization.

Organizations might throw in the inclusion and diversity policy by not implementing anything, but an organization needs to take charge. Gradually eliminating the workplace bias about women, race, culture, nationality, age, and other factors is a great way to start the inclusion process.

Culture

Culture plays a significant role in conflict resolution, especially in a diverse community such as an organization. Culture transcends the modalities of nationality, race, or language. It is how people identify themselves and attach meaning to their experiences. For conflict resolution to be improved, employees need to understand the cultural environment of the other party. An essential feature of culture in conflict resolution is employees' need to undergo conflict resolution training regularly. You might be wondering why? Now, culture is dynamic and ever-changing. For instance, you will discover that part of our way of life ten years ago has become obsolete, and new traditions have been emanated. Technology has also altered the way people perceive culture these days. Hence, these changes are also prevalent in the workplace. For employees and management to stay abreast of cultural nuances globally, they have to train themselves continuously. Organizations will always grow; you cannot stop having people from Europe, Asia, Africa, or the Middle East. Understanding different aspects of people's culture is a great way to enhance Conflict-IQ™ and equip yourself with conflict resolution skills.

Therefore, all employees must be aware of their colleagues' cultural disposition to make things a lot easier when working. In a family bound by blood, there is always conflict. In a diverse community with people from different backgrounds, there will be conflict. Employees, therefore, need to have an empathetic look at their colleague's culture and beliefs. Another critical aspect of learning and understanding other colleagues' cultural nuances is the non-verbal cues culture breeds. There are different non-verbal cues in hand movements, head movements, and understandable silence. All these cues mean other things depending on the context that they are used. Understanding the cultural environment can only be achieved through practical training in conflict resolution and actively paying attention to other people. Awareness is an integral part of forming a mutual understanding with a person from another culture. Removing any form of prejudice about that person because of the culture will also allow employees to appreciate the culture and work better.

16

Who Are You Going to Call?

> *"If we manage conflict constructively, we harness its energy for creativity and development."*
>
> —*Kenneth Kaye*

This chapter seeks to explain the essence of having specialized and trained professionals to help deal with different organizational conflict types. When conflicts arise for these kinds of people, they call on anyone to help solve them. This is where you hear stories like, "Hey, Andrew, you are good people, right? See if you can talk to Hannah." Although people skills are part of the conflict resolution package, that does not make up the entire discourse's entirety. Conflict resolution entails different aspects that require specialized and trained professionals to help improve the way employees and the organization deal with conflict.

Days will come that the conflict is much bigger than having

people skills but adopting specific techniques to resolve matters. At that stage, who do you call? If the only person the employee wants to talk to is the management, Andrew will be helpless if he just has people skills. As important as it is for organizations to hire the right employees, there is a need to consider conflict resolution as an integral part of the Human Resources department.

In our discussion on engagement and how it pays for an organization to engage its employees, we talked about one of the people you can call when there is a regular conflict occurrence. Management due to the complexities of culture in the workplace, it is expedient for them to invest in professionals that help find solutions to interpersonal, intercultural, gender, salary, and other forms of conflict.

This chapter is also vital in explaining conflict resolution in an organization. There are different types of conflicts among employees. It has been said that conflict differs in context and participants. Ultimately, the conflict resolution skill that an employee used to solve an issue might not be the same to apply if there was another conflict. Even if the issues were similar, the mere fact that there are different participants involved changes the conflict's dynamics.

So, who do you call when the same tactics do not work all the time?

The United States Bureau of Labor Statistics reports that there will be an increased number of jobs related to conflict resolution. It further shows the numbers will experience a 10% increase between 2016 and 2026, which is higher than some other professions. This statistic shows how essential professionals in the conflict resolution field are to an organization's growth.

Professionals such as arbitrators, mediators, conciliators have a tremendous impact on the organization they work with. They also organize training for employees and management to imbibe conflict intelligence as part of their organizational culture. It is necessary as once employees can resolve conflicts on their own, there would be increased productivity in the organization.

It is gratifying for many professionals in conflict resolution careers to help organizations deal with issues and equip them with the tools to get to the bottom of their problems and solve them. The sheer joy that beams through their heart is beyond exciting; the organization benefits immensely from these professionals. They are faced with different issues daily, which entails them digging deep into utilizing conflict resolution skills. Most organizations need assistance with issues that consume time and have been recurring. These professionals help show organizations the root causes of the conflict after carefully studying how they interact and work. The solutions come after the observation and conduction of interviews with employees and the organization's management.

Professionals in conflict resolution can function in an organization's Human Resources department as they can be called upon to help resolve conflicts within a department. Also, they help develop conflict management systems for the organization, which will serve as part of the culture that employees must adapt to grow.

Mediators and conflict resolution coaches utilize different skills in ensuring the peace and tranquility of an organization. Their negotiation, persuasion, and problem-solving techniques are always second to none. Immediately they show up, they assess the situation and make informed decisions based on the skills they have garnered over the years.

Also, active listening is part of their bag of tricks, as some might call it. The power of listening in an organization is even more evident at the disposition of mediators and other conflict resolution specialists. For example, for engagement coaches, the need for minorities to pour out their hearts on issues that have been a problem for them for so many years requires active listening. This is not listening to give a response but to show empathy and stand by that person. Conflict resolution is one of the most demanding career paths for many people because it involves digging up past events shaped to be the issues and contributing factors in the conflict.

After a heated argument, let us look at this scenario, which is only average in an organization filled with intellectuals. Two employees of different races are the parties involved. The argument becomes louder with each passing minute. Suddenly, one of the parties involved makes a statement, "That is why people never wanted your kind around in the first place." You can imagine the outrage that will follow. Therefore, the conflict resolution specialist needs to understand what it means to feel that way. Sometimes, this must be done delicately. Most times, the professionals brought in to speak to employees can relate to their issues. It allows the employee in question to connect better and freely with someone they are comfortable with. Nevertheless, active listening plays a vital role in fishing out the root cause and proffering the necessary solutions.

Critical thinking and reasoning are part of the arsenal of the conflict resolution specialist. They never assume anything about the conflict. They are like internal private investigators looking for traces and clues that will lead them to uncover the organization's problems.

Duties of Professionals Within the Conflict Resolution Industry

The art of conflict resolution is a broad subject that involves a host of different segments that employees need to understand.

Professionals that organizations hire in the HR department help improve and facilitate communication between two or more conflicted people in the organization. As conflict resolution experts, this is one of their principal duties. It is worthy of note that these professionals take courses on conflict resolution and have practiced for many years before being hired. These professionals are proficient in fostering relationships no matter the conflict that exists among the employees. They do this to assess the situation, understand the conflict's context, and proffer solutions while considering the parties involved.

Also, professionals in conflict resolution work as mediators who help ensure the clarity of all parties involved. Based on their experience and mastery of communication and psychology, the mediators are trained to communicate correctly, allowing each employee or party to recognize their roles in the conflict.

They also help evaluate the relevant documents and implement pertinent laws that ensure conflict resolution is imbibed in the organization like a culture. They must provide a stable platform for conflict resolution to operate; they ensure that the management and employees know the conflict resolution technique and patterns the organization needs to adopt. The policy of inclusion, diversity, and equity is one such policy that helps mitigate crises in an organization. This means that all employees should be included in the organization's activities and decision-making process, regardless of their differences. This policy accommodates the workforce as part of the organization's thinking no matter how diverse they are in culture, language, identity, race, age, and gender. This means that all employees have the same rights to opportunities and benefits attached to employment, promotions, and other activities in an organization. It puts the organization on its toes and compels them to hire people based on qualifications and merit. These hiring and promotion processes are done despite the diversity that exists in the workforce. Organizations hire people not because of their skin color but based on their expertise. Employees perform much better when there is a level playing field in the organization.

Case Evaluation

This is where conflict intelligence professionals examine the evidence, whether through observations, conducting interviews, focus group discussions, questionnaires, and other types of surveys. Consequently, conflict resolution experts seek to address the issue after the relevant information has been gathered about the conflict. It takes the professionals' discretion to address the issue by talking to each party privately or holding a session where both parties are involved. Either way, the professional is heavily involved as a neutral third party.

Conflict Coaching

This aspect is one of the most fundamental areas in conflict resolution in an organization. Management has to understand that it goes beyond hiring people full-time to solve their interpersonal conflict that emanates within the organization. This can be a bit strenuous considering the number of employees some organizations have. Conflict coaching is an area where the professionals teach and train employees on the various conflict resolution techniques and the best ways to interact with each other. In the previous chapter, we looked at how important it is for an organization to have an engagement coach. Empowering the employees to function as mediators makes a lot of sense for organizational growth. The improvement in character and disposition among the employees is an art because conflict resolution experts take the job in the first place. They believe that no one is beyond change. Therefore, seeing people transform into mediators through rigorous self-awareness and adopting conflict resolution skills is a thrill for all involved.

Mediation

The goal of conflict resolution is to guide employees to a settlement that appeals to both parties involved. Although the employees in conflict are the ones that choose to agree, the job of the professionals is to direct them to see that their relationship is far more important than the conflict. There are different techniques involved in mediation which these professionals adapt as they try to establish a common ground with the parties involved. Mediators help to reduce the cost and time of a legal issue between employees or management and employees. Arbitrators are also part of the mediation process. They stand in the gap for employees to reach an agreement with management to avoid a strike or other demonstrations. Arbitrators are the best bet for organizations when the conflict hits the ceiling with tempers flaring and employees refusing to work. Corporations employ this set of conflict resolution mediators, schools, agencies, and other organizations to help reduce the crisis's effect. They are hired to reach an agreement that both parties can agree on.

The safest option for organizations to evade any dent in their reputation is hiring a conflict resolution mediator. They function in different capacities, just as explained above. Some counselors help to provide insight and solutions to employees facing issues in the organization. Like the on-site therapist, they are ready to listen to the employees' problems and offer solutions when it matters the most. These counselors are part of an employee-assisted program. They give counsel to issues that bother employees in an organization. It is imperative to have these people in the company. There is no way an employee can fully function with problems weighing on their minds. The remedy might just be talking about the issue before it escalates.

But why wait till there is an issue before hiring a conflict resolution mediator? With the way the world is changing, there are more global companies with a diverse workplace filled with many cultures. Misunderstandings will happen from time to time; therefore, having a standby professional help mitigate the crisis will be best for its growth. The conflict resolution mediator helps to teach strategic skills and improve the organizational culture to handle issues better.

17

Re-tooling the Brain Behavioral Transformation A World of High Conflict-IQ™

> "A good manager doesn't try to eliminate conflict; he tries to keep it from wasting the energies of his people. If you're the boss and your people fight you openly when they think that you are wrong--that's healthy."
>
> —Robert Townsend

There is no way readers can create an environment that enhances employee participation and improved overall performance without developing a high Conflict-IQ™ .

Throughout this book, we have seen conflict arising in an organization is as inevitable as the sun rising every day. It is a regular occurrence that cannot be avoided, no matter how hard the organization tries. However, if all employees and management have the correct principles, tactics, and implementation to counter the crises, there would be increased productivity.

You have to bear in mind that developing a high Conflict-IQ™ is beyond resolving conflict in the organization. It transitions into improving the organization's bottom line, keeping the employees happy, and increasing productivity. Many employees find solace in understanding that no matter the issues in their organization, there will always be a solution. In that kind of setting, there is no limit to what can be achieved as a unit and individually.

Unfortunately, not many leaders and organizations have adopted the Conflict-IQ™ methodology as part of their operation mode. Others do not believe in it as a means to an end, which translates to the fact that they do not see the need for implementing Conflict-IQ™. Sadly, leaders prefer their workplace environment to have an ambiance of falsehood where people internally hate each other but smile openly because of the job. This is why you see and hear employees complain and lament about their jobs and their management. It may often not be about the salary but the organizational culture that harbors many fears and unresolved issues. This situation plagues any organization and hinders any form of progress.

Inactive leaders, who shy away from resolving issues no matter the size, create a toxic environment for the employees. Most times, the organization shuts down or loses many trusted employees because they were complacent about dealing with issues. However, if leaders have sufficient training that helps develop their conflict resolution skills, there would be an immense improvement in employee satisfaction and overall performance. Conflict resolution entails understanding the different types of conflict that can and will emanate in an organization. In diversity, leaders should endeavor to have a fair understanding of the employees' cultures. Management staff should be delegated to ensure the equitable treatment of all employees regardless of their cultural orientation.

Therefore, this chapter seeks to reveal a world where leaders with high Conflict-IQ™ can influence their employees and how this relationship can yield tremendous success from the organization. But first, let us look at ways through which leaders can develop Conflict-IQ™ .

Approximately $359 billion is the amount organizations lose annually to conflict (Creighton 2019). People attribute the issues in the organization to employees not being committed or not getting along. However, the majority of the problems that affect the organizations come from the leaders. It may be directly or indirectly and through their actions or inactions. The leaders in the organization set the tone for the culture that the employees will adopt. If the leaders lack Conflict-IQ™, the organizational culture will be in chaos. Therefore, here are some areas where leaders can develop Conflict-IQ™, especially in such a dynamic world we currently live in.

Servant Leadership

Servant leadership entails resolving conflicts before they even get to the surface. This form of training bothers the proactiveness and the ability of the leaders to read between the lines. Servant leadership teaches leaders how to be more vigilant and pay attention to the organization's employees and other aspects. For example, when a leader notices that the employees lack motivation, fun exercises can help take the edge of things and put them back into the work groove. This is taking control of the situation before it escalates. Lack of motivation can cause reduced productivity and poor performance, culminating in an uproar in the organization. Servant leadership also teaches leaders to recognize the efforts of outstanding people and employees. The support of the employees helps to motivate others to do even better.

Emotional Intelligence

Emotional intelligence and Conflict-IQ™ go hand-in-hand, and it is necessary for ensuring effective communication in the workplace. The ability to sense the deep feelings and understand each employee's emotions or parties involved in conflict sets the tone for the resolution. Here, leaders are taught that they should make the employees realize that the conflict is not worth losing a relationship for. The leader ensures a positive rapport among the employee through emotional intelligence.

Transparency

Some leaders feel that the more they appear rigid and unapproachable, the more they will respect them. But this cannot be further away from the truth; there is no better way of reaching out to your employees than being transparent. If you want respect as a leader, you have to show the employees you are willing to help. A conflict is less likely to happen when the employees can speak freely to the leaders and the management about an issue that concerns them in the workplace. Imagine the cost you are saving when all you need to do is invite the employees to your office and settle the issues just by talking.

The Role of Conflict Resolution in Solidifying Relationships in the Organization

There is only so much that leaders can do on their own in an organization because without the employees pulling their weight, the goals and objectives of the organization become redundant. Therefore, creating an environment that offers employees a good ambiance free from conflicts and issues is key to their progress.

Employees look up to leaders to take action when necessary to intervene in a matter. Where the leader is inactive, the employees become helpless and find it difficult to trust the leaders. When leaders lose their employees' trust, everything begins to go south from there; there will be no participation or motivation to work. Conflict-IQ™ helps to position leaders at the right time to solve the issues that have been affecting the employees. Recognizing the best time to act is a trait leaders get from developing Conflict-IQ™ . There are some conflicts where the best time to intervene could be when you hear the case. As the leader, you might need to get more information to intervene or understand your message's deliveries are functions of good conflict resolution skills. Leaders need to realize that no conflict has the same techniques; they may be similar. Still, conflict resolution techniques enable you to decipher the best ways to approach an issue. You could draw from past experiences, but it is not guaranteed that the same methods you used back then will suffice for this crisis. Therefore, developing Conflict-IQ™ allows leaders to be versatile and innovate ways to intervene in issues.

Conflict-IQ™ entails the leaders getting to know the employees, their weaknesses, limits, tendencies, and triggers. Leaders need to understand the dangers of overstepping their boundaries even if they know the employees personally. Of course, there are perks to this scenario, but the demerits, if manifested, can be devastating. Conflict-IQ™ gives the leaders the ability to maintain a safe distance from the employees and not become biased in issues. Imagine that if people know you are always biased when it comes to a particular employee, there would be more conflict. In essence, you and the favorite employee will be the target of many issues. The best way to get to know employees without prejudice and bias is by having open interactive sessions with every staff member. Here, you reinforce the performance expectations and how they are faring. It allows them to realize that there are things more important than conflicts. Leaders with high Conflict-IQ™ can guide and instruct employees to continue giving them a renewed focus.

An aspect of conflict resolution that resonates deeply with successful leaders is their ability to respect their employees' differences. Respecting the individualistic uniqueness of each employee as opposed to sidelining them can foster greater participation and relationship. Everyone is a product of many cultures and interactions; with the right management, employees have what it takes to improve an organization's state. It only takes the proper oversight to bring out these qualities. However, the leaders need to ensure that the employees are made to feel free in their space. With the prevalence of many different changes in culture, there are areas where leaders need to embrace the differences of the employees. The world has evolved, and a lot of cultural ideas have been incorporated into the corporate world. The diversity among the employees should be respected and harnessed to bring out the best in the people. Remember the chapter that talked about diversity and inclusion? Well, it is a part of the conflict resolution training that leaders need to subscribe to. To get the best out of a multicultural workforce, leaders need to give employees equal opportunities to showcase their talents and impact the organization as a whole.

Conflict resolution allows leaders to see issues and crises as an opportunity to grow and build new relationships with the employees. Therefore, leaders need to take the bull by the horns and face the tension without any fear. There may be some decisions that will not go down well with the employees, but as long as the situation is handled correctly, there will be peace. Leaders will know what is best for the employees since they have a good relationship with them. This is one of the reasons why some employees stay in organizations for more than twenty years. By applying attention to the needs of the employees, the conflict gradually begins to depreciate. Leaders cannot solve all the issues employees have at the same time. But the gradual answers to their problems endear the employees to the leaders.

A Whole New World

This is not a tribute to the famous Aladdin song where both the princess and the supposed prince float on the magical carpet throughout the city. This section tells a tale of how leaders and employees can work together in peace and harmony. So how does being knowledgeable in conflict resolution help organizations? Aside from the apparent reason that the absence of conflict increases productivity and the organization's revenue generation capabilities, with sufficient knowledge in conflict management, leaders can work well with employees to attain the great height that matches their goals and objectives.

Another reason why conflict resolution is necessary for the leaders and the whole organization, it establishes a solid organizational culture that is unmatched and ensures participation. An organization is filled with people from different cultures and backgrounds. For example, the salary increment is a great way to engage the employees and meet their needs, thereby ensuring tranquility and greater participation.

Leaders with high Conflict-IQ™ are invested in solving any conflict in the organization. As they solve issues with the employees, they build a formidable relationship with them. The leader has to maintain their relationship despite the crisis that comes through their doors.

Imagine a world where conflicts are met with open arms and smiling faces because it has no place to stay in an organization. In this world, leaders and employees can put on their big boy and big girl shoes to stand for the organization's established and vital principles. A world where ego and power are not the gain but ensuring every employee and staff find work thrilling.

This is a whole new world that is achievable and attainable, with leaders and employees taking conflict resolution training as part of the organizational culture. It needs to be engraved in organizations' policy that everyone needs to be skilled in conflict resolution. No conflict is more significant than the organization.

Conclusion

——

An unusual cool breeze in fills the room as I add this note here in the Silicon Valley area, in California. I have realized that even the best organizations with top-notch employees fall victim to the negligence and omission of conflict resolution in their operations.

The afterthought of regret for not resolving that issue with the board or the employee plagues many leaders today. Conflict resolution is a necessity in the dynamic workplace in any part of the world. Therefore, the only way to harmonize their culture and turn it into viable resources is upgrading Conflict-IQ™ and offering conflict intelligence as a program in the organization.

Conflict resolution is the key that unlocks the door of organizational prosperity and freedom. It is the missing link that connects employees to their motivation and the light that directs the leaders.

It is unlikely that I will find a topic as satisfying as conflict resolution; this discourse has shaped my childhood. There is a need to adopt conflict resolution as an indelible feature, to uncover the veil from organizations' faces,

As I have realized that life is about establishing and maintaining relationships, I have learned to appreciate the subject of conflict intelligence. The essence of speaking the truths in this book is to enhance organizations' operations and empower the employees.

My delight will be seeing organizations consider conflict resolution when hiring employees, ensuring that it becomes a training platform that separates the professionals from the amateurs.

References

Bolton, R. 1979. Ph.D. People Skills, How to Assert Yourself, Listen to Others, and Resolve Conflicts https://www.washingtonpost.com/news/answer-sheet/wp/2017/12/20/the-surprising-thing-google-learned-about-its-employees-and-what-it-means-for-todays-students/

Bureau of Labor Statistics .2019.
  https://www.bls.gov/charts/american-time-use/emp-by-ftpt-job-edu-h.htm

Bureau of Labor Statistics. 2020. https://www.bls.gov/news.release/wkyeng.nr0.htm

Carucci. R. (2018). 3 Ways Senior Leaders Create a Toxic Culture.

Case Studies for Conflict Resolution: A key element in civil rights training: Wisconsin WIC

Church, A. H. (1997). Managerial self-awareness in high-performing individuals in organizations. Journal of Applied

Psychology, 82, 281–292.

Conflict in a positive, respectful, and mutually beneficial way. (Ohio State University Extension)

Creighton, K. (2019). 4 Ways to train Your Leaders in Conflict Resolution and Management. From https://hrdailyadvisor.blr.com/2019/05/15/4-ways-to-train-your-leaders-in-conflict-resolution-and-management/

Darlington. R, How to Resolve Conflict – Advice on resolving differences and managing Conflict between individuals, small groups, and organizations.

Emma, S. (2019). Book Summary: The 7 Principles of Conflict Resolution by Louisa Weinstein.

Emmons, A., R. (2005). Thanks! How Practicing Gratitude Can Make You Happier. ISBN: 978-0-547-08573-9

Folger, J.P., Baruch, Bush, R. A., Della, Noce, D. K.(2010). Tranformative Mediation: A Sourcebook Resources for Conflict Intervention Practitioners and Programs.

Greenberger, D, Padesky, C. (2016). Mind over Mood: Change how you feel by changing the way you think.

Hayes, J. (2008, July). CPP Global Human Capital Report (2008), Workplace Conflict and How Businesses Can Harness it to Thrive. Retrieved July 14, 2015, from
http://img.en25.com/Web/CPP/Conflict_report.pdf

Kabat–Zinn. J. (1996). Wherever You Go, There You Are: Mindfulness Meditation in Everyday Life Resolving Conflict Constructively and Respectfully – Tips on how to manage and resolve.

Kegan, R. 1982. The Evolving Self, Harvard University Press.

Kegan, R. 1994. In Over Our Heads. Harvard University Press.

Kegan, R. 2009. Immunity to Change. Harvard University Press.

Kogan, B. E (2020). 3 Effective Strategies to Manage Workplace Conflict. From https://blog.dce.harvard.edu/professional-development/3-effective-strategies-manage-workplace-conflict

Larcker, D., Miles, S., Tayan, B., & Gutman, M. (2013). 2013 Executive Coaching Survey. Retrieved September 10, 2015, from http://www.gsb.stanford.edu/faculty-research/publications/2013-executive--survey

Maslow, A. 1976. Further reaches of human nature. New York: Viking Press

Mayer, B. (2004, July). Beyond Neutrality. Retrieved October 14, 2015, from https://www.mediate.com//articles/mayerB1.cfm

McAdoo, B., Welsh. N., & Wissler. R. (2003). Institutionalization: What do empirical studies tell us about court mediation? Dispute Resolution Magazine.

Moore, W., Christopher (2014). The Mediation Process, Fourth Edition: Practical Strategies for Resolving Conflict

Mouser, D. (2018). Workplace violence. Mouser Law firm, PC.

Robins, S. (2002). A consultant's guide to understanding and promoting emotional intelligence in the workplace. In Lowman, R. (Ed), Handbook of Organizational Consulting Psychology. John Wiley & Sons, Inc.

Shipper, F., & Dillard, J. E. (2000). A study of impending derailment and recovery of middle managers across career stages. Human Resource Management, 39, 331–345.

Taylor, S. N., Passarelli, A. M., & Van Oosten, E. B. (2019). Leadership coach effectiveness as fostering self-determined, sustained change. The Leadership Quarterly, 30(6).

ABOUT AUTHOR

—

Yvette Durazo, MA, ACC, is the principal consultant of Unitive Consulting, a workplace organizational effectiveness, strategic conflict management, and leadership development firm. Yvette brings innovative techniques to promote a positive workplace culture in organizations to encourage trust, productive human capital engagement, and inclusion. Clients benefit from her wealth of knowledge and professional experience in the art of building a trusting workplace relationship. Some of her services include training, mediating conflicts in the workplace, anti-bullying prevention, settlement negotiations, developing dispute system design, and bringing unique strategies to address the Diversity, Equity, and Inclusion (DEI) workplace.

Yvette is passionate about optimizing professionals and teams to engage in constructive problem-solving communication toward instilling respect, civility, and collaboration. She believes that human conflict is one of the most important things organizations must learn to work with and harness to overcome any derailing of employees' performance and engagement. Her methodologies are like a vitamin that is the breath of life to the immunity of organizations.

Presently, Yvette is an instructor for the Human Resource Management Certification program at the University of California, Santa Cruz Extension Silicon Valley and for the University of California, Davis, Continuing Education, Conflict Resolution Program. She also teaches undergraduate and master's degree students for Portland State University courses in Mediation Skill. She holds an ACC coaching credential from the International Coach Federation, a master's degree in Conflict Resolution, Negotiation, and Peacebuilding from California State University Dominguez Hills, and an undergraduate degree in International Business from San Diego State University. She is certified in Human Resource Management, Mediator, Restorative Justice Facilitator, Project Management, and is a non-violence communication specialist. She is a former Core Adjunct Professor at National University, where she taught courses in Alternative Dispute Resolution, Mediation, and Communication for over six years, and a former Instructor for the Leon Guanajuato Mexico Institution Power of Justice. She is also the former ADR Program Administrator for the Superior Court of California, Alameda County. Yvette is fully bilingual in Spanish and has expertise in cultural diversity and inclusion. She can be reached at unitiveconsulting@gmail.com and you can follow her work at https://www.unitiveconsulting.com | https://www.conflictintelligentbook.com

Made in the USA
Middletown, DE
18 September 2021